DISASTER IN DAMP SAND

The Red River Expedition

CURT ANDERS

GUILD PRESS OF INDIANA

Library of Congress
Catalog Card Number
97-77772

ISBN 1-57860-015-4 hardcover
ISBN 1-57860-016-2 paperback

Manufactured in the United States of America.

Text design by Sheila G. Samson

Also by Curt Anders:
   Fighting Confederates (1968) G. P. Putnam's Sons
   Hearts in Conflict: A One-Volume History of the Civil War (1994)
   Birch Hill

CONTENTS

ILLUSTRATIONS

Major General Nathaniel P. Banks, USV
Senator Benjamin F. Wade
Major General Henry W. Halleck, USA
Lieutenant General Richard Taylor, CSA
General Edmund Kirby Smith, CSA
Rear Admiral David Dixon Porter, USN
Major General Frederick Steele, USV
USS *Carondelet*
Congressman Daniel H. Gooch

MAPS

Trans-Mississippi Battle Area
Banks Abandons the Red
Mansfield and Vicinity
Sabine Crossroads
Pleasant Hill
Porter's Skedaddle
Banks' Escape from Grand Ecore
Monett's Ferry
Arkansas Battle Area
Jenkins' Ferry

Maps by Joan Pennington based on sketches by the author.

FOREWORD

Anyone making a list of neglected Civil War subjects would have to place near the top the importance of bodies of water—rivers, inlets, creeks, harbors, bayous—in shaping the decisions and actions of commanders. The presence or absence of water often determined strategy and tactics. Ulysses Grant owed much of his early fame to his adroit use of the Mississippi, Tennessee, and Cumberland rivers. Union war managers named field armies and many battles for rivers.

Indeed, some streams seemed to take sides. The York in Virginia was a valuable federal supply route. And in 1864 Louisiana's Red River was clearly pro-Confederate: In no other major operation during the war was the lack of water more critical to the outcome than it was to the Red River Campaign.

"This expedition presents many remarkable features," wrote Senator Benjamin F. Wade in the majority report of the investigation made by his Joint Congressional Committee on the Conduct of the War. That was a gross understatement. No other federal operation west of the Mississippi involved so many gunboats and transports, or thousands of troops, or artillery pieces. And seldom, if ever, during the Civil War did decisions made and actions taken during a single and relatively brief campaign blight and wreck the careers of so many leaders of both sides.

Remarkable, in particular, is the probability that no campaign of this magnitude has been so neglected by so many historians and students of the Civil War for so many years.

Are not disasters among life's most fascinating events? Aristotle called attention to the dramatic impact of the fall of important people from prosperity and acclaim. There is even a hint of the supernatural in the baffling behavior of the Red River—and also perhaps in the unseen, ghostly hand of Jackson guiding his former disciple, Richard Taylor.

Those neglectors who are pro-North may have found the facts emerging from the Red River Expedition excessively unsettling. Here, Abraham Lincoln reached beyond his grasp. Lax overall Union management of this portion of the war effort justified the efforts made by "Bluff Ben" Wade and his fellow inquisitors to find and condemn the rascals responsible for the fiasco. And, of course, the ending of this story was an embarrassingly unhappy one for the North.

But it hardly seems likely that even after the passage of more than 130 years, pro-Confederates' nerves are still so raw because of the Yankees' appalling misconduct that they would deny themselves the therapeutic pride they are entitled to take in Dick Taylor's mauling of the invaders. This repulse, moreover, was the last significant, clear-cut Confederate victory in the war.

This study of the Red River Expedition is the first freestanding one to appear since 1959, when Ludwell H. Johnson's *Red River Campaign: Politics and Cotton in the Civil War* became the standard source. But what sets this narrative apart?

Here, the focus is more on the military developments—the thinking (or lack of it) behind them, the balances struck between principles or theory and geographic and other aspects of combat realities, and the lessons to be learned from the experiences of ordinary men on both sides who were obliged to cope with extraordinary challenges.

More use is made herein of the participants' own words, taken mainly from the official records of the Union and Confederate armies and navies, and the report issued by Senator Wade's committee which contained the testimony of witnesses called before it. While some of the quoted passages may seem long and at times tedious, they are as close as we can get to what our predecessors really thought, said, and claimed they did in circumstances that were unique in this nation's history.

Some of those words' spellings have changed as we have moved from ironclads to spacecraft, and not all are marked [sic]. Most, especially those in extracts from official records, appear as they were set down.

At bedrock, here we have the elements of the only stories William Faulkner thought worth telling—stories that "help man endure by lifting his heart, by reminding him of the courage and honor and hope and pride and compassion and pity and sacrifice which have been the glory of his past."

ACKNOWLEDGMENTS

All of us who have studied the Red River Expedition owe an enormous debt to Ludwell Johnson, but no one is as beholden to him as I am—or more grateful. Also, I wish to thank the Library Committee of the Union League Club of New York for giving me access to their splendid civil War collection; the Desmond-Fish Library in Garrison, New York, for obtaining books for me through the Mid-Hudson Library loan network; and the Library of the United States Military Academy at West Point, New York. The folks at Guild Press of Indiana—Nancy Niblack Baxter and Sheila Samson in particular—deserve my special thanks. And *muchas gracias* to Joan Pennington, who graciously made time to produce the maps.

CHAPTER 1

THE WEAVING OF A TANGLED WEB

Washington, D.C., The Capitol, December 14, 1864
Joint Congressional Committee on the Conduct of the War
Testimony of Major General Nathaniel P. Banks

Major General NATHANIEL P. BANKS sworn and examined.
  By the Chairman, Mr. Wade:

Question: *What is your rank in the army?*
Answer: *I am a major general in the volunteer army.*
Question: *Have you been stationed in New Orleans, in command of that department?*
Answer: *Yes, sir; the Department of the Gulf, including Louisiana, Texas, and portions of Alabama and Florida.*
Question: *How long have you been in command of that department?*
Answer: *I assumed command on the 16th of December, 1862.*
Question: *You succeeded General Butler in command of that department?*
Answer: *Yes, sir.*
Question: *Are you still in command of that department?*
Answer: *Yes, sir; on leave of absence.*
Question: *Will you now proceed to give the committee, in your own language and in your own way, a narrative of what is known as the Red River expedition or campaign? I will ask, from whom did you receive your orders in relation to that campaign?*
Answer: *From General Halleck, then general-in-chief, and subsequently from Lieutenant General Grant, when he became general-in-chief.*
Question: *Can you furnish the committee with copies of the orders which you received from those generals?*
Answer: *I have not all the orders with me, but I will forward them to the committee.*
Question: *Will you state now the substance of those orders, according to your best recollection, about what time you received them, and, also, what you did in reference to them?*

1

Answer: It will be necessary for me to refer to operations in which I was engaged previously to that, in order to give a full understanding of the case.

Question: Do so; make your statement in your own way.

Answer: Port Hudson surrendered on the 9th of July, 1863 . . .[1]

<hr />

The Joint Congressional Committee on the Conduct of the War was established in December 1861 to investigate the causes of the Union defeats at Bull Run in July of that year, and at Ball's Bluff in October, and other matters of concern to the federal legislators. The CCW's powers were quite broad. It could and did hold secret hearings in a room in the Capitol's basement, which brought to mind the Star Chamber proceedings in medieval England.

Witnesses were not allowed to be accompanied by counsel or anyone else. Subjects of the CCW's inquiries were denied the right to cross-examine those who had testified against them. All who appeared before the CCW were admonished to remain silent regarding what had transpired during their interrogation. The committee made reports exclusively to Congress and only when it chose to do so.

Congress had not been in session in mid-April 1861, when Union Major Robert Anderson's surrender of Fort Sumter opened the Civil War. Newly inaugurated President Abraham Lincoln set restoration of the Union as the federal war goal and used his Constitutional authority as commander-in-chief to quell the "rebellion."

However, many members of Congress—particularly those who were zealous in their advocacy of slavery's abolition—found Lincoln's measures too timid. Senator Edward D. Baker of Oregon, for example, declared: "We may have to reduce them [the seceded states] to the condition of territories, and send from Massachusetts or Illinois governors to control them." Thaddeus Stevens, a congressman from Pennsylvania, called for the South to be "laid waste and made a desert." Radical Republican lawgivers returning to Washington that December for the reconvening of Congress were also irate over Lincoln's selection of Major General George Brinton McClellan, a Democrat, to replace retiring Brevet Lieutenant General Winfield Scott as general-in-chief of the Union armies.[2]

Senator Baker was also a colonel commanding a brigade in Brigadier General Charles P. Stone's division, which had been placed along the Potomac River's Maryland shore across from Virginia's Loudoun County. McClellan involved Stone's forces in an abysmally directed reconnaissance that led to a Union defeat on October 21, 1861, at Ball's Bluff on the Potomac. In this fight Baker was killed.[3]

In their reports Generals McClellan and Stone suggested that the late colonel/senator had made egregious blunders. Formation of the Committee on the Conduct of the War, then, was an action taken partly through grief over a fallen colleague and deep craving for punishment of McClellan and Stone, and also to wrest direction of the war from the Executive branch in general and from Abraham Lincoln in particular.[4]

Said Senator Henry Wilson of Massachusetts: "We should teach men in civil and military authority that the people expect that they will not make mistakes, and that we shall not be easy with their errors." Thus was born, historian T. Harry Williams would write a century later, "the unnatural child of lustful radicalism and confused conservatism."[5]

From the outset the seven-member joint committee was bipartisan in theory but clearly dominated by Radical Republicans. Senator Benjamin F. Wade of Ohio was chairman. As Professor Williams described him: "He was of average height, but square-built, heavy, and slightly drooped. His long white hair fell straight back from a good forehead. His complexion was clear and dark, his eyes small, jet-black, staring. His jaw protruded aggressively and his upper lip doubled at the corners, giving his face a ferocious appearance."[6]

"Bluff Ben" Wade's witness at the committee's meeting on December 14, 1864, Major General Banks, had moved up in life from a textile mill in Waltham, Massachusetts, where he was a bobbin boy, to two terms as the Bay State's governor and later to the United States House of Representatives where he served as Speaker. Banks was among the first politicians to be appointed major generals by President Lincoln after Fort Sumter; until early in 1864 he outranked even Ulysses S. Grant. Certainly, he *looked* the part of a commander, even though he was often referred to as the "Bobbin Boy."

"A newly cultivated mustache added dignity to Banks' grave, handsome face," wrote his biographer Fred Harvey Harrington, "and the General dressed to absolute perfection. Yellow gloves set off the deep blue of his uniform. His cap was set just right, his boots were highly polished, his spurs sparkled in the sunlight. Even enemies admitted that they 'never saw a more faultless-looking soldier.' "[7]

Unfortunately for the Union, however, by the time of his summoning by the Committee on the Conduct of the War in late 1864, Nathaniel Banks' record as a leader in combat was definitely *not* commensurate with his "splendid" appearance. Confederate Major General T. J. Jackson had whipped the Bobbin Boy twice in Virginia back in 1862 and had missed a third chance to maul him at Second Bull Run later that year because Banks' corps had been deemed fit only for rear-echelon guard duty during that Union defeat. His presence in Washington "on leave of absence" had been prompted by the results of his generalship during the recent Red River expedition, regarding which Chairman Wade had asked the general to "give the committee a narrative."[8]

"From whom did you receive your orders?" Chairman Wade had asked. "General Halleck," Banks had replied, and later he provided the text of the initial directive:

HEADQUARTERS OF THE ARMY,
Washington, D.C., November 9, 1862.

GENERAL: *The President of the United States having assigned you to the command of the Department of the Gulf, you will immediately proceed, with the troops assembling in transports at Fort Monroe [Virginia], to New Orleans, and relieve General Butler. An additional force of some ten thousand men will be sent to you from Boston and New York as soon as possible.*

The first military operations which will engage your attention on your arrival at New Orleans will be the opening of the Mississippi and the reduction of Fort Morgan [Alabama] or Mobile city, in order to control that bay and harbor . . . As the ranking general in the southwest, you are authorized to assume control of any military forces from the Upper Mississippi which may come within your command. The line of division between your department and that of Major General Grant is therefore left undecided for the present, and you will exercise superior authority as far north as you ascend the river.

The President regards the opening of the Mississippi river as the first and most important of all our military and naval operations, and it is hoped that you will not lose a moment in accomplishing it.

This river being opened, the question arises how the troops and naval forces there can be employed to the best advantage. Two objects are suggested as worthy of your attention:

First, on the capture of Vicksburg, to send a military force directly east to destroy the railroad yards at Jackson and Marion, and thus cut off all connexion by rail between northern Mississippi and Mobile and Atlanta . . .

Second, to ascend with a naval and military force the Red River as far as it is navigable, and thus open an outlet for the sugar and cotton of northern Louisiana . . .

It is also suggested that having Red River in our possession, it would form the best base for operations in Texas.

* * *

These instructions are not intended to tie your hands or hamper your operations in the slightest degree. So far away from headquarters, you must necessarily exercise your own judgment and discretion in regard to your movements against the enemy, keeping in view that the opening of the Mississippi River is now the great and primary object of your expedition . . .[9]

H. W. HALLECK
General-in-Chief

General Halleck's order was lengthy and rather tedious, but it was straightforward. By contrast, in early November of 1862 Abraham Lincoln was having to resort to duplicity and subterfuge in a vain attempt to please all of the people all of the time.

For many months New England textile mill owners and abolitionists had been demanding that he send an expeditionary force to recapture Texas. Concurrently, out in the "Old Northwest"—Minnesota, Wisconsin, Illinois, Indiana, and Ohio—politicians were applying pressure on him to reopen the Mississippi River, blocked at the time by strong Confederate fortresses at Vicksburg and Port Hudson (in northern Louisiana). Because 1862 had been marked by Union defeats in the Shenandoah Valley of Virginia, in the Seven Days battles east of Richmond, and along Bull Run for the second time, Lincoln was in no position to satisfy his constituents in both regions. Yet he could not afford to lose the support of either one.

New England's advocates of the Texas invasion could trace the roots of their argument to the period between the Mexican War and Fort Sumter. Opponents of slavery believed that if large numbers of Yankees of their persuasion moved to Texas and settled there, these transplanted farmers would be able to demonstrate that free labor could produce more cotton, and at lower cost, than slave labor; as a result, when this theory became widely known and acknowledged, slavery would wither and die.[10] Having a dependable supply of low-cost cotton was of great importance not only to all New Englanders who had stakes in the textile industry, but to the economy of the entire Northeast.[11]

In his *Journey Through Texas*, published in 1857, Frederick Law Olmstead described the success of anti-slavery German immigrants who had settled in the central portion of the state.[12] Later, New England's abolitionists would be favorably impressed by the fact that in Texas' February

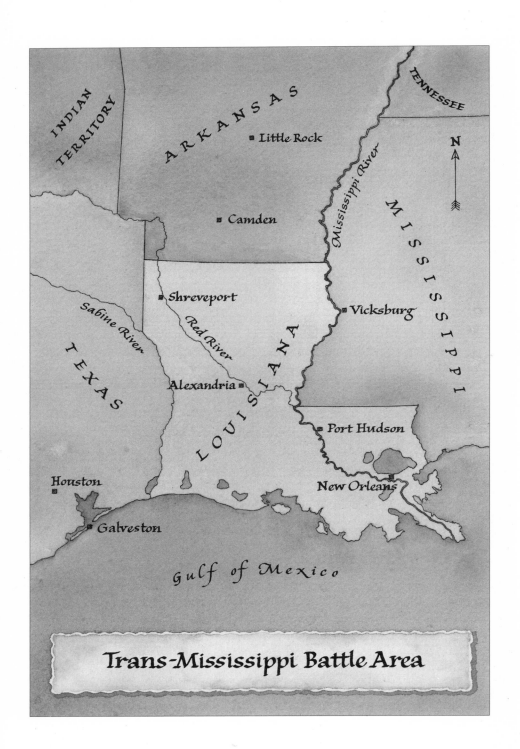

Trans-Mississippi Battle Area

1861 secession referendum, virtually all of the votes cast opposing with-drawal from the Union came from Central Texas counties in which these strong believers in performing, themselves, whatever farm and ranch labor might be required in order to survive and prosper, were in the majority.[13]

To this convergence of interests (eliminating slavery and obtaining plentiful supplies of low-cost cotton) the fact of civil war added an addi-tional argument and a means of attaining their goals. Texas ought to be conquered, many advocates of such an operation urged, because of the state's strategic location and value to the Confederacy; and troops to do this might be drawn from New Englanders who would be promised land in exchange for their military service.

Edward Atkinson, in an 1861 pamphlet entitled *Cheap Cotton by Free Labor*, asked:

Have not our soldiers a right to demand as their best compensation for sub-duing the rebellion, that at least one small portion of the country which they will restore to the Union shall be kept open to them for peaceful occupation?

And, anticipating the Radical Republicans several years later, Atkinson added:

The question may well be asked whether the confiscation of the lands of all rebels—individuals and states—and the bestowal of them as a bounty to our soldiers is not a necessary first step in the reconstruction of southern so-ciety which must be accomplished, to render the reconstruction of the Union solid and enduring.[14]

Among the early advocates of an invasion of Texas was Major General Benjamin Franklin Butler, a politician who like Nathaniel Banks had been governor of Massachusetts and who possessed no military qualifications whatsoever. As had Banks and other "political" generals Abraham Lincoln had appointed, Butler saw the war as an opportunity to follow Generals George Washington, Andrew Jackson, and Zachary Taylor into a postwar presidency.[15] And as a Massachusetts man, he was familiar with the promptings of Olmstead and Atkinson. But General Butler was something of a thinker (or at least an adapter), and in January 1862 he shared an idea with newly appointed Secretary of War Edwin McMasters Stanton.

Butler suggested that he be given enough troops to make a landing on Texas' Gulf of Mexico coast and drive toward San Antonio, while another Union force started southward from Kansas to combine with him in crush-ing and seizing the state. But Stanton was too new to his secretaryship to know where priorities belonged, so launching his idea was as far as Butler got.[16]

Two months earlier, however, Commander David Dixon Porter had presented Secretary of the Navy Gideon Welles with a proposal designed to capture New Orleans, a port the Union's blockade had not been able to close. New Orleans was the Confederacy's largest city. Moreover, it could serve as a base for future efforts to reopen the Mississippi to federal shipping from the Great Lakes to the Gulf and also cut the Confederacy in two—to carry out the second goal General-in-Chief Winfield Scott had proposed in his ridiculed "Anaconda" strategy.[17]

President Lincoln approved the Porter proposal. The expedition, under the command of Rear Admiral David G. Farragut, included transports carrying about five thousand soldiers destined to serve as General Butler's army of occupation once New Orleans was captured.[18]

New Orleans came under Union control on April 27, 1862, with General Butler as commander of the federal Department of the Gulf.[19] Whether or not Lincoln's purpose in sending this utterly incompetent officer so far away from Washington was to minimize the damage the former Massachusetts governor could do, Butler soon acquired the nickname "Spoons" because the disappearance of silver and other valuables from the home in which he was quartered. Louisiana's military governor was also known as "Beast" Butler because of the harshness and alleged corruption of his administration.[20]

However, while New Orleans' seizure was being planned and even after it became a fact, managing the war in the East had been President Lincoln's main concern. "The people are impatient," the frustrated commander-in-chief had complained to Quartermaster General Montgomery Meigs in mid-January 1862. "[Secretary of the Treasury Salmon P.] Chase has no money, and tells me he can raise no more; the General of the Army [McClellan] has typhoid fever. The bottom is out of the tub. What shall I do?"[21]

Lincoln allowed McClellan to move his huge Army of the Potomac from the Washington area down its namesake river and Chesapeake Bay to Fort Monroe at the tip of a peninsula about eighty miles southeast of Richmond. But the "Young Napoleon" had already proved he could not command an army in the field *and* direct the operations of all the other Union forces, so in late March the President relieved him as general-in-chief and assumed that duty himself.[22] During his conduct of the Union's response to Confederate Major General Thomas J. "Stonewall" Jackson's Shenandoah Valley Campaign in May and June of 1862, Lincoln proved that he could not "do it all," either: Jackson whipped him.

Superb generalship and the heart-stopping audacity displayed by General Robert E. Lee and "Stonewall" led to a series of Confederate victories in the summer of 1862. In late August and early September Washington itself was in danger of being captured.[23] Even so, the amount of cotton obtained in Louisiana after New Orleans' seizure having been disappointing, together with the failure of efforts to wrest from the rebels control of the Mississippi from above Vicksburg southward to Baton Rouge, politicians in both New England and the upper Midwest demanded that Lincoln return his attention to their regions' plights.

Declared Governor Richard Yates to the Illinois legislature:

Can it be for a moment supposed that the people of the valley of the Mississippi will ever consent that the great river shall flow for hundreds of miles through a foreign jurisdiction, and they be compelled, if not to fight their way in the face of the forts frowning upon its banks, to submit to the imposition and annoyance of arbitrary taxes and exorbitant duties to be levied upon their commerce?[24]

At about the same time, Governor John A. Andrew of Massachusetts was again viewing with alarm the idleness of roughly two-thirds of the spindles in the Bay State's mills due to the sharp drop in supplies of cotton. Texas ought to be conquered, he reiterated, and newspapers supporting abolition, confiscation, and Yankee colonization agreed.[25]

Abraham Lincoln's ability to respond affirmatively to these regional complaints, however, remained severely limited. Back in late 1861 General McClellan had maintained that the Union had no troops to spare for operations in Texas or Louisiana. In 1862, through the battle fought in mid-September along Antietam Creek east of Sharpsburg, Maryland, Lee's Army of Northern Virginia had thinned eastern Union armies' ranks by more than fifty-two thousand men.[26] If more were to be done to please the two dissident regions, where were the large numbers of soldiers such ventures required to be found?

"Political" Major General John A. McClernand, a friend of Lincoln's from Illinois, thought he had the answer. Let me recruit and train fresh forces from the Old Northwestern states, he asked the President in effect, and lead them down the Mississippi to clear it.

Whether Lincoln recognized it or not, the plan reflected McClernand's own presidential ambitions, his belief that minuteman-type troops commanded by officers drawn from civilian occupations were far superior to "elitist" West Point-educated leaders, and his dislike of Major General Ulysses S. Grant in particular. Lincoln told McClernand to go ahead—despite the fact that Grant and Major General William Tecumseh Sherman were even then preparing to launch drives aimed at taking the batteries frowning from the bluffs at Vicksburg out of the war.[27]

Having done this much to placate the Old Northwest, Lincoln returned his attention to the anguish of cotton-starved New England. Governor Andrew, in Massachusetts, offered to raise troops for Texas' conquest and noted that his predecessor, Major General Banks, was available to command them—Banks' whippings by Jackson in Virginia earlier notwithstanding.[28]

"Thus Lincoln's response to his two problems was an attempt to solve both at once," wrote historian Ludwell H. Johnson a century later.[29] General McClernand's recruits, said *The New York Times*, "will feel a personal interest in its success, because to a certain extent the pecuniary prosperity of every one of them will be found dependent on the unobstructed navigation of the Mississippi River." By way of balancing, and echoing earlier abolitionist dogma, the *Times* added: "Texas needs to be colonized as well as captured."[30]

Union Secretary of War Edwin Stanton made Lincoln's solution official in October 1862 by authorizing Banks to establish a "headquarters in New York to organize a Southern expedition."[31] From this document's ambiguity sprang the assumption that Banks' destination was some point along Texas' four-hundred-mile coastline. So prevalent was this reaction that Indiana's Governor Oliver P. Morton was provoked into sending Lincoln a long letter that began with "The fate of the North-West is hanging in the balance" and included, near the end, this sharp warning:

> *And I give it here as my deliberate judgment, that should the misfortune of arms, or other causes, compel us to the abandonment of the War and the concession of the independence of the Rebel States, that Ohio, Indiana, and Illinois can only be prevented, if at all, from a new act of secession by* [another] *bloody and desolating Civil War.*[32]

This and other indications that Lincoln could not please all of the Union's self-centered regions all of the time led him to change his mind. But he allowed the idea that Texas was indeed Banks' destination to proliferate and persist. Not until mid-December 1862, when General Banks' transports reached New Orleans did even the Texans who had accompanied him on the voyage from New York learn the truth. In fact, Banks had been sent not to conquer Texas but to replace Butler as commander of the Department of the Gulf and to employ the untrained troops Andrew had recruited for him to cooperate with Grant in regaining control of the

Major General Nathaniel P. Banks, USV

Vicksburg-Port Hudson stretch of the Mississippi River.[33]

Judicious if subtle statecraft, Morton and other Old Northwesterners might have termed Lincoln's decision to give priority to reopening the Mississippi; *despicable dastardly duplicity*, is how the infuriated Texan Unionists—understandably—characterized it. In a foolish and feeble attempt to cleanse themselves of alleged sin, the federal war managers had Banks land a small force on Texas' Galveston Island. It was summarily repulsed.[34]

And so it was that 1862 ended with Radical Republicans enraged because Lincoln had sacked Butler and had apparently blighted the abolitionists' and textile industry stakeholders' hopes of colonizing Texas with free laborers who might grow cheap cotton on confiscated land. But 1862 had not been a good year for Lincoln and the Union in any case. Underscoring the point, on December 13 General Lee's Army of Northern Virginia had wrecked a series of gallant but ill-conceived and ultimately futile attacks thrown by Major General Ambrose E. Burnside against nigh-impregnable Confederate defense lines along Marye's Heights, just west of Fredericksburg, Virginia—in the process killing, wounding, and capturing more than 12,600 Yankees.[35]

If the desires of the Old Northwest seemed to have prevailed over those of the New Englanders, however, such impressions were premature. In December General McClernand marked his successful recruiting of Midwesterners by taking to wife a lady said to be his sister-in-law and going on a two-week honeymoon. In his absence, prompted by General-in-Chief Halleck, Ulysses Grant ordered "Cump" Sherman to go to Memphis, load McClernand's troops on transports, steam down the Mississippi, and seize Chickasaw Bluffs, just north of Vicksburg, while he drove southward through central Mississippi toward the "Gibraltar of the West."[36]

Both Union attempts failed. In coming months at least seven other tries by Grant to remove Vicksburg from the war would fail. But there was no need for Halleck to provide Nathaniel Banks with fresh orders: "Old Brains" had said everything the situation required—and that it would require—in his instructions dated November 9, 1862.

⊰—⋯—⊱

During General Banks' interrogation by the Committee on the Conduct of the War on December 14, 1864, he had responded to Chairman Wade's prompt, "make your statement in your own way," by stating that "Port Hudson surrendered on the 9th of July, 1863." Actually, he was beginning his narrative *in medias res*. Much had happened between his arrival in New

Orleans late in 1862 and the point from which he described some of his subsequent actions. None of it reflected credit on the Waltham Bobbin Boy.

As General Halleck had perhaps inadvertently forecast in the orders he gave Banks on November 9, 1862, high if not highest on the Union's 1863 military objectives priority list was the reopening of the Mississippi—specifically, elimination of the Confederate fortresses at Vicksburg and, roughly 110 miles downstream, Port Hudson. Halleck had protected and guided Ulysses Grant through McClernand's challenge; thereafter, Washington looked to Grant to seize Vicksburg. But Port Hudson was in Louisiana, and therefore in Nathaniel Banks' Department of the Gulf.

Viewed from Washington, more than a thousand miles distant, all that General Banks appeared to have to do was move enough troops from New Orleans up the Mississippi to Baton Rouge, only twelve miles or so south of Port Hudson, seize the rebel fortress, and then steam up the river to assist Grant in taking Vicksburg. Because Port Hudson seemed likely to fall first—its defenses were not as formidable as those of the Gibraltar of the West—this strategy seemed both prudent and feasible. Theoretically, Banks' forces outnumbered the rebels in Port Hudson's garrison by more than three-to-one. And the navy's Mississippi Squadron could provide covering fire from Admiral Farragut's gunboats as Banks' divisions closed in on their objective.[37]

Before Banks could move northward from New Orleans, however, complexity proliferated. Confederate Major General Richard Taylor returned to Louisiana from service under Stonewall Jackson in the Shenandoah Valley Campaign, where Taylor had routed Banks' forces in a battle fought south of Winchester and had driven them in panic all the way to safety in Maryland. Once recovered from an illness that had taken him out of the war in Virginia, Dick Taylor gathered loose bands of Texans and Creoles into a rabble large enough to strike a federal installation west of New Orleans and to arm itself with weapons and ammunition looted from its arsenal.[38] This came as a rude shock to the Yankees, who had assumed that virtually all of the Confederacy's soldiers in Louisiana were committed to defending Port Hudson. Next, in mid-March Admiral Farragut was able to get only his flagship USS *Hartford* and one other vessel past surprisingly devastating fire from Port Hudson's batteries.[39]

General Taylor's intent in raiding Banks' outposts had been to restore Louisianans' terribly depleted morale as a step toward boosting recruiting and support, not necessarily to fight a battle of attraction similar to the one his mentor Jackson had conducted (with Taylor's assistance) nearly a year earlier in Virginia's Shenandoah Valley. But Banks, who may have recalled

Senator Benjamin F. Wade

the thorough beating Taylor had given him at Winchester, dared not undertake the upriver movement to attack Port Hudson with so able an enemy on his flank. Instead, he sent his units westward and then northeastward in a vain attempt to annihilate Taylor.[40]

Nathaniel Banks' preference for what he called this "eccentric movement" appalled General-in-Chief Halleck. Old Brains was "exceedingly disappointed" and he reminded Banks that *opening the Mississippi . . . has been continually presented as the* first *and* most important *object to be attained. Operations up the Red River, toward Texas, or toward Alabama, are of only secondary importance, to be undertaken* after *we get possession of the [Mississippi]*."[41]

The chase, which cost the Union army roughly six hundred casualties, ended on the Red River at Alexandria, the geographic center of Louisiana. Banks paused long enough to send southward to New Orleans more than two thousand wagons loaded with cotton and other captured commodities which he valued at $3 million.[42]

By intimidating Banks and luring him away from Port Hudson, Taylor delayed the Yankee force so long that Grant had stopped expecting help from Banks and had gone ahead with his Vicksburg campaign. Although some of the Union war managers thought Grant ought to send a corps down to support Banks' belated attempt to take Port Hudson, he decided to concentrate on his own objective.[43]

The Confederacy's war managers in Richmond thought it best for Taylor to march eastward from Alexandria to the Mississippi near Vicksburg in the hope of preventing Grant from moving troops down the river's west bank beyond the reach of the fortress' guns. Taylor tried, but he arrived too late and with too weak a force to achieve anything.[44] In the meantime, Banks completed his plundering at Alexandria and put his troops on transports for the ride down the Red River to its junction with the Mississippi, a few miles from Port Hudson.[45]

By May 27, 1863, General Banks was ready to assault the defenses of the objective he had been told months earlier to take. He had a three-to-one numerical advantage. His attack would be supported by heavy gunfire from Admiral Farragut's gunboats. And Confederate Major General Franklin Gardner seemed most unlikely to be able to hold everywhere along a four-and-one-half-mile line that had been prepared for three times the number of defenders he had.[46]

But the orders Banks issued were vague. Two of his three division commanders, he wrote, were to "dispose their troops so as to annoy the enemy as much as possible during the cannonade, by advancing skirmishers to kill the enemy's cannoneers and to cover the advance of the [third?] assaulting column. They will place their troops in position to take instant advantage of any favorable opportunity, and will, if possible, force the enemy's works at the earliest moment."[47]

Later, Banks would explain his loss of nearly two thousand men in the course of being repelled by complaining that he had not been given enough men to carry out his mission, that his subordinates' leadership was weak, and that Gardner's fortifications were too strong.[48] More difficult to justify were the results of Banks' next failure. It began on June 13 with heavy bombardment delivered by Farragut's gunboats to soften-up the Confederates' defenses. Had that not alerted Gardner and his men that battle was imminent, General Banks' demand that the rebels surrender certainly did. On June 14 when Banks launched his assaults he lost another two thousand of his men in achieving nothing at all.[49]

During this second repulse some of General Banks' officers had refused to commit their troops to the fight. Moreover, many soldiers did not advance because their nine-month enlistments were about to expire.[50] But Gardner, who had graduated four files ahead of Ulysses Grant in West Point's class of 1843, and mindful of his orders from Vicksburg's commander, Lieutenant General John C. Pemberton, to hold at all costs, led men who were determined to stop the Yankees.[51]

Stalled, Banks and his demoralized federals began siege operations. By mid-June he had lost more than forty-five hundred troops—ten times the Confederates' casualties—and was no nearer victory than he had been when he had arrived.[52]

Such results reflected the quality of Nathaniel Banks' generalship. In his first campaigns as commander of the Department of the Gulf he had been led far astray and long delayed by Taylor's rabble and he had been unable to breach fortifications defended by rebels who were trying to survive on a diet of mule and rat meat, badly outnumbered and out-gunned, unable to expect resupply of ammunition or anything else.

Along with the imminence of starvation, news from upriver that Vicksburg's Confederate commander had surrendered on July 4 convinced General Gardner that further resistance would be futile, given the imminent availability of Grant's troops to complete the work Banks had started but had not been able to finish. On July 9 Gardner offered his sword to Union Brigadier General George L. Andrews, Banks' representative at the formal surrender ceremony, but Andrews—recognizing the valor of Port Hudson's defenders—refused to accept it.[53]

"Success is a duty" had been Nathaniel Banks' motto from his days in the textile mills,[54] but *save the surface and you save all* might have been more apt—or so the language in his reports to the Union's War Department suggested. "The siege will be remembered not only for its important results," he wrote, "but also for the manner in which it was conducted."[55]

Well, not quite: Major General George G. Meade's defeat of Lee's Army of Northern Virginia on July 4, 1863, at Gettysburg, Pennsylvania, had somewhat eclipsed Grant's having accepted the Vicksburg garrison's surrender on the same day, and the capture of the Gibraltar of the West denied all but scant attention to Banks' victory at Port Hudson and "the manner in which the siege had been conducted."

From the Bobbin Boy's point of view, that might have been a blessing; reports of his incompetence as a combat commander would be crowded out in the North by publicity devoted to gloating over other Union armies' twin successes at Gettysburg and Vicksburg.

It was understandable, then, that in December 1864 General Banks chose to begin his narrative as he testified before the Committee on the Conduct of the War by referring to his July 1863 victory. Port Hudson's surrender, however, had in fact marked the end of one phase of the struggle for control of the vast region the Confederates called the Trans-Mississippi and the beginning of another and—for Nathaniel Banks—a far more challenging one.

+══──══+

After Port Hudson's capitulation, General Banks told the Committee on the Conduct of the War, "I joined in a recommendation to the War Department that I should be allowed to make a movement against Mobile, stating my general reasons for it . . . This recommendation was forwarded the last of July or the first of August. I received instructions from the War Department that my military reasons for this campaign were approved, but that there were political reasons, not given to me in detail, but, as I supposed, growing out of European complications, requiring that the flag of the United States should be immediately re-established in Texas. Everything was left to my discretion, but my instructions were imperative to raise our flag in Texas in the least possible time."[56]

So the general testified on December 14, 1864, but again he had given only a partial report.

Nathaniel Banks and his officers and men had not been able to pause at Port Hudson for celebration of their victory because Richard Taylor and his rabble were reported to be driving toward the Mississippi to prevent the Yankees' return to New Orleans.[57] Actually, jerking Banks around Louisiana like a neutered wildcat on a leash was about all Stonewall's disciple had been able to try, given the vast discrepancy between the numbers of men under his command and those of his enemy.

And so, for a while, matters would remain. Banks made it back to his New Orleans base. Taylor reverted to his practice of striking Union forces wherever they could be hit, mainly (as before Port Hudson) west of New Orleans.

General Banks' near-term goal, opposing and if possible eliminating Taylor, was mostly to provide security for his headquarters city and base of operations. But, as he told the Committee on the Conduct of the War, he expected to be given the seizure of Mobile as his next objective.[58]

Now that the second element of former General-in-Chief Winfield Scott's Anaconda proposal—opening the Mississippi all the way to the Gulf—was a reality, the Union's war managers were preparing to move on to the third: application of pressure on the eastern half of the Confederacy. Such a task was thought to be easier because the flow of supplies and other support from the Trans-Mississippi had been stopped.[59] Major General William S. Rosecrans had neared Chattanooga in early July and it seemed possible that he could drive on southeastward to Atlanta. If Banks could seize Mobile, an advance launched northeastward from that base could—at a minimum—attract Confederate strength from Rosecrans' front.

So plausible did this strategy seem, Banks eagerly awaited word of its adoption. Instead, from General Halleck came a message sent from Washington on August 6:

> There are important reasons why our flag should be restored in some part of Texas with the least possible delay. Do this by land, at Galveston, at Indianola, or at any other point you may deem preferable.

And Halleck closed by reiterating: "There are reasons why the movement should be as prompt as possible."[60]

That this abrupt change in signals may have been rooted in a decision with which Halleck disagreed became apparent four days later when he telegraphed Banks that the order he had sent on August 6 "was of a diplomatic rather than of a military character, and resulted from some European complications, or more properly speaking, was intended to prevent such complications." Then he added:

> In my opinion neither Indianola nor Galveston is the proper point of attack. If it is necessary, as urged by Mr. Seward, that the flag be restored to some one point in Texas, that can be best and most safely effected by a combined military and naval movement up the Red River to Alexandria, Natchitoches, or Shreveport, and the military occupation of northern Texas.

"I write this simply as a suggestion," the general-in-chief concluded, "and not as a military instruction."[61]

Banks had not had much opportunity to learn the fine points of dealing with the high command. He and Halleck had nothing in common beyond the color of their uniforms. Also, Halleck hardly ever did more than *suggest*, holding that a general in the field is the best judge of what is to be done.

Nathaniel Banks took Halleck at his word. On August 26 he registered his disagreement:

To enter Texas from Alexandria or Shreveport, would bring us at the nearest [to points that] *are accessible only by heavy marches, for which the troops are hardly prepared at this season of the year; and the points occupied would attract little attention; and if our purpose was to penetrate farther into the interior, they would be exposed to sudden attacks by the enemy*
. . .

In any case, Banks noted, water in the Red River was too low for gunboats and transports to reach Alexandria. Turning to the order to plant the flag somewhere in Texas, he proposed seaborne shipment of troops and a landing near the mouth of the Sabine River. From there the Union forces would move overland to Houston and Galveston.[62]

Ironically, Banks may have known more than his superior in Washington about the reasons for both the dashing of his hopes regarding Mobile and the urgency of the need to plant the Stars and Stripes in Texas. As the senior Union official in New Orleans he was the State Department's *de facto* representative; and as such, he maintained cordial relations with key diplomats in the French, Spanish, and British consulates.[63] Accordingly, he may have been well aware of what had been happening in Mexico when, on August 10, General Halleck telegraphed him that the order he had sent on August 6 "was of a diplomatic rather than of a military character."

Back in 1859 when Benito Juarez seemed to have won a civil war in Mexico, the United States promptly granted his government diplomatic recognition. But measures promulgated by Juarez angered the Spanish, British, and French, who vented their ire by putting armed forces ashore at Vera Cruz in December 1861—at a time when the United States was in no position to aid Juarez by enforcing the Monroe Doctrine.

Soon the Spanish and British abandoned the effort, which had been launched in large part to collect debts the Mexicans had incurred during their revolutions. But the French not only stayed but added forces and advanced toward Mexico City.

Emperor Napoleon III nourished a dream of French domination of Latin America. Mexico's location made it an ideal base from which other invasions could be launched. And beset as he was by a rebellion in his own bailiwick, it seemed that Abraham Lincoln could do nothing to prevent the consignment of the Monroe Doctrine to history's ash can.

But as Hernan Cortes and Winfield Scott had learned much earlier, the French expeditionary force's commander found that it was no easy thing to advance under fire for roughly two hundred and seventy miles from Vera Cruz on the Gulf Coast to the capital the Aztecs had called Tenochtitlán, climbing to altitudes of more than fourteen thousand feet along the way. By May 5, 1863, at around the time Nathaniel Banks was finally doing something about Port Hudson, the French had reached Puebla; on June 10 they entered Mexico City; and by early August they had chased Benito Juarez' troops northward almost to the Rio Grande border with Texas.[64]

Such was the background for Secretary of State Seward's prompting of Lincoln and Halleck to order Banks to plant the flag in the Lone Star State. Halleck had only scorn for mere gestures, as the tone of his messages to Banks reflected. But the former Speaker of the House of Representatives understood Washington politics better than Halleck; as he was getting whipped during the Shenandoah Valley Campaign more than a year earlier, Banks had told a subordinate: "We have more to fear, sir, from our friends than the bayonets of our enemies!"[65]—and good soldier that Banks was trying to be, he turned to the flag-planting task he had been given.

Low water levels in Louisiana's stretch of the Red River having precluded General Banks from adopting Halleck's suggestion that he take that route into Texas via Shreveport, Banks developed a plan of his own. It called for the seaborne movement of troops to a landing site near Sabine Pass, the mouth of the river that divided that part of Texas from Louisiana. Once ashore, Major General William Franklin would lead the five thousand men he had brought there on transports overland west-southwestward to Houston and then southeastward to Galveston.[66]

Four gunboats escorted Franklin's steamers to their common destination. On September 8, the naval vessels moved within the range of six light guns at a fort manned by fewer than fifty men commanded by Texan Lieutenant Dick Dowling, in happier times a Houston saloonkeeper. In a short but sharp duel three of the Yankees' gunboats were hit. Two were disabled, ran aground, and surrendered; the other two returned to the troop-laden transports, which Franklin ordered turned back toward New Orleans.[67]

Seldom in history had so few men defeated so many in so short a time.

"I cannot explain what happened," General Banks told the committee. He then described a futile attempt to reach Texas by moving westward on land from New Orleans and his success in establishing a Union beachhead near Brownsville, at the southern end of the Texas coastline.

Banks' Sabine Pass operation might not have ended in such embarrassing failure had he been able to assign the mission to a man abler than Franklin. However, and curiously, both the Union and the Confederacy had been making the rebel Trans-Mississippi and federal Department of the Gulf dumping grounds for officers whose performances in the battles fought in the east had been disappointing, or (as in Dick Taylor's case) who had been transferred westward to recover from illness or wounds.[68]

General-in-Chief Halleck was generous in dismissing Franklin's humiliating repulse at Sabine Pass by noting that the objects of Banks' expedition were political rather than military.[69] As late as mid-October, however, Banks was still plaguing Washington with speculation regarding what might have been achieved had Franklin reached Houston with his five-thousand-man force instead of getting whipped at Sabine Pass by less than fifty Texans.[70]

Soon Banks returned to the idea of moving up the Red River. He was willing to try it, he said, but that route would require a march of "between four hundred and five hundred miles." Moreover:

The enemy destroying all supplies as he retreats, and the low stage of the water making it impossible for us to avail ourselves of any water communications . . . it would require a communication for this distance by wagon trains. Later in the season this can be done, making Alexandria the base of operations; but it could not be done now. The rivers and bayous have not been so low in this State for fifty years.[71]

Banks defended his Sabine Pass decision in a message to the President, informing him also that he intended to try to put troops ashore at some other point along the long Texas coastline. Back on August 15 he had told General Halleck that he would "plant the flag in Texas within a week." Two months and two weeks later, on November 2, 1863, a seaborne force led by Banks delivered the Stars and Stripes in a landing made near Brownsville and the mouth of the Rio Grande.[72]

In fact, the delay had made no difference; French power and momentum in Mexico were such that even the success of General Franklin's botched Sabine Pass operation within a month would have had no significant deterrent value.[73] Even so, emboldened perhaps by his success in occupying

Brownsville, Banks ordered landings at several other sites between the Mexican border and Galveston that were thought to be lightly defended. At a minimum, these beachheads provided Banks with the opportunity to appoint generals he wished to exile to command them.[74] But after only a few weeks these detachments proved to be more expensive than they were worth, and by early 1864 all but the one at Brownsville had been withdrawn.[75]

⊹⊱══⊰⊹

Whether or not the efforts to do something about Texas had been much ado about nothing, during the time General Banks' attention had been directed to those projects Abraham Lincoln had been doing a great deal of thinking about how the Southern states then in rebellion might be restored to their *status quo ante bellum*. And as a result, the Union's president was about to turn Karl von Clausewitz's observation that war is the extension of politics by other means on its head: Louisiana, Lincoln had decided, was as good a place as any to find out if politics might be the extension of *war* by other means.

Since the Shenandoah Valley Campaign in May of 1862 the Union's President had been well aware of Nathaniel Banks' inadequacies, but he had tolerated the general's most recent military lapses because he had plans that required political skills he knew the onetime Speaker of the U.S. House of Representatives possessed. Lincoln, mindful that 1864 would be a hotly contested presidential election year, foresaw that likely campaign issues would include procedures for bringing back into the Union the states that had resisted federal coercion by seceding. And he needed Banks' help in applying his approach to restoration.

Even though the war was far from won, in December 1863 Lincoln issued a Proclamation of Amnesty and Reconstruction which offered a plan that would enable the "erring sisters" to return to the family bosom. Louisiana, the President believed, provided a good opportunity to test the policies he had suggested. Also, it was possible for that state's government to be installed and a new constitution to be adopted before the Republicans convened in June 1864 at Baltimore to renominate him or replace him with some other candidate for the presidency. And Abraham Lincoln was too astute a politician to overlook the three electoral votes he might gain from restoring Louisiana to statehood—votes he might need to win in the November 1864 election.[76]

And so it was that Lincoln called upon Nathaniel Banks to add a political responsibility—direction of an experiment designed to determine the kind of future millions of people in the defeated South would have—to his other burdens: command of military operations along the Gulf coast from the Rio Grande to Mobile Bay, and administration of a state in rebellion. Could the Bobbin Boy carry such a load?

Curiously, Nathaniel Banks thought he had as good a chance as Abraham Lincoln or anyone else to be elected president, possibly in 1864.[77] To achieve that goal, however, Banks would have to win victories over the rebel forces in his Department of the Gulf and obtain the Confederate cotton idle mills in New England needed so desperately—*and* to make certain newspapers and the voters gave him credit for these accomplishments.

Ambitions apart, it had to be nigh-impossible for a president in Washington and his creature in New Orleans to deal with each other on an accurately informed basis. This distance-imposed impediment was nothing new and it was not unique. Indeed, a year earlier it had compelled General-in-Chief Halleck to admonish Lincoln that "a General in command of an army in the field is the best judge of existing conditions."[78]

In any case, by November 7, 1863, the Union's President found it necessary to write Banks—who was down at Texas' southernmost tip at the time—to complain that "nothing was being done" in New Orleans. In his reply General Banks claimed that he was "only in partial command," adding: "There are not less than four distinct governments here claiming . . . independent powers based upon instructions received directly from Washington, and recognizing no authority other than their own."[79]

Since Banks had proved unable to stop the bickering among the contending factions, President Lincoln gave him extraordinary power to administer political programs. These included registration of voters who had taken a loyalty oath, scheduling an election in February to elect a new governor, and election in March of delegates to a convention that would write a new constitution.[80]

"Time is important," Lincoln had stressed, preparing as he was to issue his Proclamation of Amnesty and Reconstruction in early December when Congress reconvened. And Banks heeded Lincoln's admonition, though the political tasks the president had given him would cause many delays in preparing for the Red River campaign General-in-Chief Halleck had been advocating since November 1862.

Abraham Lincoln considered Arkansas another state ripe for restoration, and he gave Major General Frederick Steele the mission of guiding the local authorities through the process.[81] Steele was an able warrior, a graduate of West Point, veteran of hard fighting in the Mexican War, among the few who held the regular army together between the wars, the survivor of a number of battles in this one. Yet Steele's service had all been in the West where valor and competence drew much less attention than they did in the East. And for all his merit, he was commanding a small force in a region generally considered a backwater of little importance.[82]

The lure of Arkansas' electoral votes brought Halleck's Red River proposal out of its pigeonhole. Initially, Halleck seemed to have envisioned the seizure of Shreveport as the cutting of a major communications link between the Confederacy's vast Texas base and its eastern battle areas. This would have been in accordance with what he had written in *Elements of Military Art and Science*. But politician Lincoln was adding weight to the adoption of Shreveport as a military objective. Just as Banks needed to expand the limits of federal control in Louisiana in order to carry out the president's restoration experiment, Steele might make a greater contribution to it if he could gain control of a larger portion of Arkansas—specifically its southwestern quarter. If Steele's and Banks' forces converged at Shreveport, federal troops could then move westward from there into Texas with the Red River their supply line and New Orleans their base.

And so it was that the thinking of Lincoln the would-be candidate meshed with that of military theoretician Halleck. But General Banks appeared to be preoccupied by his manifold responsibilities in New Orleans, and as 1863 neared its close he seemed no more interested in a Red River campaign than he had been a year earlier when Halleck had cited it as a course of action that might be taken after the Mississippi had been reopened to federal navigation.

CHAPTER 2

IT WAS IMPOSSIBLE
TO DESCRIBE WITH TRUTH

An excerpt from the testimony of Major General Banks given to the Committee on the Conduct of the War during his interrogation by Senator Benjamin F. Wade, chairman, on December 14, 1864:

In December [1863] I received a despatch from General [-in-Chief Henry W.] Halleck stating that all the western generals were in favor of a movement directly upon Shreveport, and all operations against Texas from that direction; and that as I knew, he himself had always been of that opinion. That movement had always been pressed upon me by General Halleck before I left Washington to assume command of the department . . . I had said as much [about] the difficulties of the land route into Texas as was becoming an officer of the government when he knew that the government had taken a different view of the subject.

Question: *These statements you speak of are contained in the correspondence?*

Answer: *Yes, sir, and I will transmit them to you. In addition to what I had said in my general despatches on the subject, I directed Major D. C. Houston, of the engineer corps, to prepare a memorial presenting all the difficulties of the movement against Shreveport, as well as the advantages . . . In that memorial the preparations necessary for that campaign were specially and strongly stated:*

    First. That all the troops west of the Mississippi should be concentrated for that purpose.

    Second. That they should all be put under the command of one general . . .

    Third. That considering the uncertainty of the navigation of Red River, a line of supplies be established, or preparations made for it independent of water communications; first by a train of wagons, and ultimately by a railway from opposite Vicksburg to Monroe and then to Shreveport . . . And Fourth. That preparations should be made for a long campaign, so that, if we reached Shreveport without encountering the enemy, and he receded from Shreveport, we would be able to follow him; the military being of the opinion that it was necessary to disperse or destroy that army, and not merely to take the place and hold it.

Not one of these conditions was established, and I had no power to enforce any of them. All I could do was to transmit this memorial to the government, because it embraced views that had been talked over for a year and a half by all our officers. I stated in my despatches that with the preparations contemplated by that memorial, and the forces proposed by the government, the movement against Shreveport could be effected and our success made certain, assuming that those suggestions which would occur to anybody in regard to expeditions of that kind would be carried out.

[The Confederates] had 55,000 men on their payrolls, but in reality only about 35,000 men, conscripts and all, and but about 25,000 effective men; and with the force that we would have, 35,000 to 40,000 men, under one command, with the assistance of the navy, I regarded success as certain; but all depending on that concentration.

Having stated this view, I said to the government, "I await instructions." They immediately replied, "It is impossible for us to give you instructions, at this distance, from Washington. You must communicate with General Steele and General Sherman. Everything is left to your discretion in that way . . . "

Question: *Did not this broad discretion which they gave you imply a right to command these generals to send forces to you?*

Answer: *No, sir; they were not in my command. I asked that the command should be given to some one general. But it was understood that General Sherman was to command his own troops, and General Steele was to command his. I should have acted under either one of them with perfect satisfaction . . .*[1]

―――✦―――

It was standard practice for members of the Committee on the Conduct of the War to "lead" witnesses. Persons giving testimony had no counsel, so no objection could be raised when an interrogator attempted either to put words into a subject's mouth or to give him an opportunity to say something that would tend to save or condemn himself.

Usually, the interrogations seemed directed toward documenting conclusions the Radicals had already reached. Occasionally, however, the committee devoted its hearings to the exoneration of kindred spirits who had fallen into disrepute or to the shifting of blame from one of their ilk to others, often to Abraham Lincoln.

At this early point in the committee's investigation of the Red River expedition it was not clear what Ben Wade was trying to do. Banks was an abolitionist but hardly a Radical. Were his misfortunes his own fault, or Lincoln's? Or Halleck's?

Apart from the editing General Banks was doing, some of his recollections were somewhat disingenuous. Of course, this was only natural in the circumstances. And Banks was not alone in having found General-in-Chief Halleck an unusually difficult man with whom to work; only a small number of generals, notably Grant and Sherman, not only understood Old Brains' ways but approved and admired them.

Accordingly, whether or not Nathaniel Banks' conduct in Louisiana was being judged, that of Henry Halleck most certainly was relevant.

The general-in-chief had been entirely straightforward in his orders to Banks back on November 9, 1862, in stating: "These instructions are not intended to tie your hands or to hamper your operations in the slightest degree. So far away from headquarters, you must necessarily exercise your own judgment and discretion in regard to your movements against the enemy . . ."[2] Even so, General Halleck had made references to the desirability of a Red River operation almost a standard feature of his messages to Banks. Grant and Sherman knew how to blend attention to Halleck's prods with the freedom of action he had not only granted them but had insisted they exercise; Nathaniel Banks did not.

Worse, by advocating another attempt to seize Galveston the Bobbin Boy may have compelled Halleck to abandon all hope that Banks would or could respond effectively to his suggestions. In any case, during the fall of 1863 Halleck obtained the reactions of Generals Sherman, Grant, and Steele, and Rear Admiral David Dixon Porter to the idea of making the Red River the primary line of operations. Seldom had he involved himself so deeply in an undertaking. But Banks was accomplishing nothing of value with his landings on Texas beaches and Halleck was under pressure to complete the planning for the armies' operations in 1864—operations that might include a drive to seize Mobile.

General Grant wanted no part of any "sideshow" that might divert troops from the campaigns he contemplated in the coming year.[3] Halleck responded to him in a letter dated January 8, 1864, that revealed some of the reasons a Red River venture was likely:

It was deemed necessary as a matter of political or State policy, connected with our foreign relations, and especially with France and Mexico, that our troops should occupy and hold at least a portion of Texas. The President so ordered, for reasons satisfactory to himself and his cabinet, and it was therefore unnecessary for us to inquire whether or not the troops could have been employed elsewhere with greater military advantage.[4]

General Sherman, then Grant's subordinate, had lived in Alexandria as recently as 1861—as superintendent of the Louisiana State Seminary of Learning and Military Academy—and he knew the Red River better than Banks or most other Union officers. Sherman not only endorsed Halleck's proposal but said that he would like to take part in such an operation if Grant approved. Nothing came of that; Grant sent him on a raid that took him from the Mississippi to Meridian, and Sherman had second thoughts about serving under a political general.[5]

On January 4, 1864, Halleck wrote Banks: "Generals Sherman and Steele agree with me in opinion that the Red River is the shortest and best line of defense for Louisiana and Arkansas, and as a base of operations against Texas." He also urged Banks to "communicate with them, and also Admiral Porter, in regard to some general cooperation."[6] And a week later, Halleck telegraphed Banks: "I am assured by the Navy Department that Admiral Porter will be prepared to co-operate with you as soon as the stage of water in the southwest will admit of his use of his flotilla there."[7]

Earlier, on December 23, General Banks had protested that his orders were to plant the flag in Texas, which he had done, and that water levels in Louisiana's bayous and rivers was too low for the Shreveport operation to be feasible.[8] A week later Banks wrote the general-in-chief: "It is my desire, if possible, to get possession of Galveston."[9] This was indeed curious, since Banks had been rejecting that possibility since August. He had also told Halleck that he favored the Red River alternative if the forces available to him were—in Banks' judgment—sufficient.

All of which Banks had summarized in his testimony.

However, it came as a surprise to the war managers in Washington when, on January 23, 1864, Banks set aside all his reservations in replying to General Halleck:

With the forces you propose, I concur in your opinion, and with Generals Sherman and Steele, "that the Red River is the shortest and best line of defense for Louisiana and Arkansas, and as a base of operations against Texas." . . . I shall most cordially co-operate with them in executing your orders.[10]

Senator Wade might well have asked the witness testifying before the Committee on the Conduct of the War, *Why this change in willingness?* Banks never explained it, but in a letter to the President dated February 2, 1864, he mentioned the existence of 105,000 bales of cotton under the control of Confederate officers "west of the Mississippi" and added: "In Arkansas and Texas there is probably as much more."[11] He did not send the letter, but capturing that cotton and the publicity derived from conquest of the Trans-Mississippi could give the Bobbin Boy a tremendous boost toward the presidency.

Bluff Ben Wade or one of his colleagues might also have asked General Banks, *What effect did Major Houston's "memorial" have on the thinking of the high command in Washington?*

On February 1, 1865, General-in-Chief Halleck said in a message to Banks: "The report and map contain very important and valuable information." Regarding Houston's concern over water levels, Halleck offered this counsel:

If the Red River is not navigable, and it will require months to open any other communication with Shreveport, there seems very little prospect of the requisite co-operation or transportation of supplies. It has, therefore, been left entirely to your discretion, after fully investigating the question, to adopt this line or substitute any other.[12]

For whatever reasons, General Banks remained committed to the Red River campaign. But word from General Steele was slow in coming, and not until the end of February was Cump Sherman free to visit New Orleans and work out the arrangements for the loan of troops to Banks.[13] These delays did no harm, however, since the level of water in the Red River was too low even for shallow-draft vessels and it was not expected to rise until early in March.

Banks had set March 17, 1864, as the date for Admiral Porter's gunboats to reach Alexandria. With Porter would be transports bearing ten thousand men borrowed from Sherman's force. Roughly twenty thousand men under William Franklin's command would be waiting there.[14]

Major General Henry W. Halleck, USA

Given such a plan, General Sherman imposed a limit of thirty days regarding his troops' service under Banks. His host asked him to stay for the inauguration of Louisiana's recently elected pro-Union governor, Michael Hahn, but Sherman disapproved of political activities while the war was still being fought and he returned to his headquarters.[15]

What Sherman missed, and what twenty thousand witnesses saw, was a spectacular ceremony on March 5 that included floats and banners and a rendition of the "Anvil Chorus" by more than three hundred musicians from all the bands in the Department of the Gulf's army and six thousand singing school children accompanied by the ringing of church bells and the firing of cannon by electricity. It was, Banks wrote General-in-Chief Halleck, "impossible to describe it with truth."[16]

+=-=-=+

Indeed, in his testimony on December 14, 1864, General Banks had not described with truth the opposition he expected to encounter in a drive toward Shreveport. So vast was the Confederate Trans-Mississippi, and so feeble were Union efforts to gather information, that the twenty-five thousand "effective" men Banks thought the rebels had were really only a fraction of that whittled-down figure. Moreover, apart from ordering Major Houston to prepare the "memorial," the Bobbin Boy did not seem to have made much of an effort to ascertain the conditions prevailing in the parts of his department his forces did not control.

"All we want is to be left alone," Confederate President Jefferson Davis had said in stating the South's war aims, and many people in the four states of the Trans-Mississippi felt that way about Richmond and especially Shreveport. Governors kept the few remaining able-bodied men for home guard units. Some areas were rich in food, cattle, fodder, and cotton while in others near-starvation loomed. Trans-Mississippi Department commander Edmund Kirby Smith was tolerated, but no one west of the Mississippi had asked for him and no one would have cared much if he left.

Lieutenant General Edmund Kirby Smith, a graduate of West Point in the class of 1845, won glory early in the war by leading his brigade—newly arrived by rail from the Shenandoah Valley—in an attack on the advancing Yankees' right flank just in time to contribute to the Union army's wrecking at First Manassas, as the battle along Bull Run near Washington became known in the South.[17] Knoxville was his next post; prevention of Lincoln's efforts to wrest heavily Unionist East Tennessee from Confederate control was his primary mission. Apparently, though, reports of federal vulnerability rebel cavalrymen brought back from raids in Kentucky caused

Kirby Smith's ambitions to override his appraisals of reality. Acting in "cooperation" with General Braxton Bragg, who commanded the adjacent military department, he led his troops northwestward in an invasion of the Bluegrass State that was repelled—whereupon he joined a number of other unsuccessful generals who had been exiled to the Trans-Mississippi. Edmund Kirby Smith, however, was sent westward to Shreveport, Louisiana, as commander of that military department.[18] Accordingly, conducting a successful defense of the region might restore some of the luster his military reputation had lost in Kentucky.

Within Kirby Smith's vast Trans-Mississippi Department Dick Taylor was in charge of operations in Louisiana and Sterling Price directed troops in Arkansas and (at times) Missouri. At Galveston, another general exiled from the East, Major General John Magruder, presided over shortages of everything needed for the successful defense of Texas. Because of enormous distances, roads little better than pig trails, and rivers that were obstacles to be crossed instead of watery highways, the unfortunate "Prince John" might as well have been somewhere in Asia, Sterling Price in South America, and Dick Taylor high in the Swiss Alps. And hundreds of miles separated each of them except Taylor from Kirby Smith.

Long a student of military history at places as varied as Yale, Harvard, and Edinburgh, Taylor received a graduate education while serving in the Shenandoah Valley Campaign under Jackson, his mentor.[19] Although he was the son of former President (and Mexican War general) Zachary Taylor and the brother of Confederate President Jefferson Davis' late first wife, he was—like rebel cavalryman Nathan Bedford Forrest—a natural soldier who had earned his prominence among the Trans-Mississippi's defenders. But Taylor's stake in preventing Yankee control of his homeland was personal; by the end of 1863 the war had ruined him.[20] No Confederate had more intense desire to smite the invaders hip and thigh.

The men Dick Taylor led were from farms and ranches and small towns in Texas, the winding bayous and lush prairies of central and southern Louisiana, New Orleans' streets and docks, and river ports such as Natchez. Riding horses and caring for them, firing rifles and shotguns and pistols, enduring nasty weather and frequent hunger were skills a man had to have in order to survive on what was still very much the frontier. Such men were rowdy and contemptuous of efforts to discipline them. But in fights they were superb, often driven by memories of the Yankees' wanton vandalism and awareness of the many other severe hardships the war was imposing on their loved ones.

Given the characteristics of his men, Taylor recognized the need for senior officers capable of winning and holding their obedience—like the

Lieutenant General Richard Taylor, CSA

troops, seasoned warriors who were determined to destroy the Yankee invaders so that the people of their states could get back to the pleasures of peaceful living. Those leaders he found came from a variety of backgrounds, as these examples show:

Brigadier General Jean Jacques Alfred Alexander Mouton, the son of a highly respected former governor of Louisiana, was a graduate of West Point who had been wounded at the Battle of Shiloh. Taylor put him in command of a brigade, initially, and early in 1864 he gave him responsibility for holding Alexandria.[21]

Later, when Mouton became a division commander, one of the brigades was led by Colonel Henry Gray, whose fighting had been entirely within Louisiana. Kirby Smith objected to Gray's promotion to brigadier general because of habits considered "not good," but Taylor thought him an excellent soldier.[22]

Another brigade commander was General Camille Armand Jules Marie, Prince de Polignac, born in France and a veteran of the Crimean War. Like Mouton, Polignac fought at Shiloh. Because the men in Polignac's unit, Texans mostly, could not pronounce his name they nicknamed him Polecat.[23]

John G. Walker, a native of Missouri, was commissioned directly into the regular army just before the Mexican War. After Sharpsburg in September 1862, he was promoted to major general and transferred to the Trans-Mississippi Department where he was placed in command of a division of Texas infantry. Taylor had Walker covering a line from Marksville southeastward to Simmesport on the Atchafalaya, near the place where the Red River empties into the Mississippi. A two-hundred-man detachment from Walker's command garrisoned Fort De Russy, an uncompleted fortification on a bluff overlooking a bend in the Red, that had been started by Kirby Smith over Taylor's strong objections.[24]

Perhaps the most experienced of Taylor's subordinates was Major General Thomas Green, whose first battle was San Jacinto in 1836, the fight in which Texans led by Sam Houston won the republic's independence from Mexico. Green went on to become a hero in the Mexican War and in early 1863 led a force that drove the Yankees off Galveston Island. He was among Taylor's most valued officers in the campaigns west of New Orleans in 1863. Green's cavalry division was ordered back to Texas late in that year, again to clear the coast of federals, but by March 1864 it was on its way eastward to rejoin Taylor.[25]

In contrast to Green's cavalry, Brigadier General James E. Harrison's Texans were mounted infantry and often carried out scouting missions. They were on one near Monroe, northeast of Alexandria, when Taylor assigned the regiment to Brigadier General St. John Richardson Liddell, whose small units patrolled the east bank of the Red River. A small cavalry unit led by Colonel William G. Vincent was watching the country south of Alexandria. Brigadier General James P. Major was a West Point graduate who served in the 2d Cavalry in Texas before Fort Sumter; in early 1864 he was following Green eastward to rejoin Taylor. Other cavalry leaders were Colonel August Buchel, born in Germany but later a settler in north Texas, and Colonel Xavier B. DeBray.[26]

Such were Dick Taylor's assets, but even given the best of circumstances he could not expect to have many more than ten thousand men. Banks could throw at least thirty-thousand or more at him, or so it seemed. Moreover, when the federals advanced they would be supported by limitless stocks of ammunition, food, fodder, and all the other things an army required. Taylor would have to depend on the series of supply points he had established along the high ground between the Red River and the Sabine using the loot captured from the Yankees in the 1863 campaigns against Banks' forces west of New Orleans.[27]

Both Sterling Price and Taylor had scouts who supplied them with a steady flow of reports regarding movements of Union forces and rumors of what the Yankee generals were planning. Observers in Union-occupied Memphis, Vicksburg, Natchez, and New Orleans passed along information confirming Southern suspicions that both Banks and Steele would head for Shreveport in 1864 as soon as Porter's gunboats could get above the rapids at Alexandria.[28]

Edmund Kirby Smith and Dick Taylor differed greatly in temperament and also in points of view. About the only thing on which they could reach a meeting of the minds was that there would be fighting.

Taylor's range of concerns was narrow, even parochial, which was not surprising given his background as a Louisiana planter, legislator, and leader of the state's troops in battle and his assignment as commander of the West Louisiana District. Yet he genuinely believed and argued with vehemence bordering on insubordination that destroying Banks' army ought to be the main object, one toward which all of the Trans-Mississippi Department's resources should be committed. Moreover, during the Shenandoah Valley campaign in 1862 Taylor had found Banks to be an indecisive and ineffective combat leader and he expected him to prove equally inept again.[29]

Edmund Kirby Smith, however, was acutely aware of the complexities involved in both obtaining support from the governors of four states and pro-Confederate tribes in the Indian Territory and defending the entire Trans-Mississippi region. Officials in the area regarded him as Richmond's man, a well-meaning person but one who could do little or nothing to benefit them.

Shreveport, however, was completely under Kirby Smith's control; naturally he tended to see the Banks-Porter-Steele combination primarily as a threat to his headquarters, which he may have considered a symbol of his ability to carry out his nigh-impossible mission. Also, Kirby Smith envisioned a textbook response to the Yankee challenges: concentrating his forces and employing them to crush one drive, then turning to demolish the other—thus punishing General-in-Chief Halleck for ignoring Napoleon's warning against attempting to combine separated elements of an army on a battlefield in the face of an enemy.[30]

But operating on the basis of theory was a luxury Kirby Smith could not afford. Perhaps worst of all, he gave the impression he was unable to stick with a decision once made. For a time he seemed to agree with Taylor that Banks should be dealt with first. Then he declared variously that Steele's weaker force would be easier to beat and also that Steele posed a greater threat. He infuriated Taylor by indicating at one point that he meant to abandon Shreveport—and all of Louisiana and Arkansas—and lure the Yankees to destruction in East Texas.[31] Such mental meandering drove the well-read and impatient Taylor to refer to department headquarters as "Hydrocephalus at Shreveport," and he admonished his superior to quit wasting time:

Action, prompt, vigorous action, is required [he wrote]. *While we are deliberating the enemy is marching. King James lost three kingdoms for a mass. We may lose three states without a battle.*[32]

+⟝═⟞+

Washington, D. C., The Capitol, January 6, 1865
Joint Congressional Committee on the Conduct of the War
Testimony of Major General Wm. B. Franklin

Major General WM. B. FRANKLIN sworn and examined.
By the Chairman, Mr. Wade:

Question: *What is your rank and position in the army?*
Answer: *I am a major general of volunteers, and a brevet brigadier general in the regular army. I am now the president of the board for retiring disabled officers, in session at Wilmington, Delaware.*

Question: Were you in what is known as the Red River expedition, under
             General Banks, in the spring of 1864?
Answer: I was in that expedition.
Question: Please state, in your own way, what connexion you had with
             the expedition, and whatever came under your observation dur-
             ing the expedition that you deem material.
Answer: During the winter of 1863 and 1864 I had some conversation
             with General Banks on the subject of an expedition by way of
             Shreveport to Texas. I understood that he favored such an ex-
             pedition. I gave to him what I thought were very good objections
             against it. The main objection I urged was the fact that the Red
             River was not certain to rise in the spring. Another objection
             was, that the road from Shreveport to Houston, where we
             would be likely to first meet the enemy in force after leaving
             Shreveport, was nearly 300 miles long, and was destitute of
             provisions and forage, and I did not think it possible to march
             an army of the size and kind he wanted to take through that
             country. He told me he was sure the river would rise, and that
             the country he was sure would support an army between
             Shreveport and Houston. I then went back to Franklin [Louisi-
             ana], where my troops were; I then received orders to move
             about the 12th of March . . . General Banks first informed me
             that he had promised to meet General Sherman's forces at Al-
             exandria on the 17th of March. This information I received on
             the 10th of March. As Alexandria was 175 miles from
             Franklin, of course it was impossible to fulfill his promise, so far
             as my troops were concerned.[33]

However, back on December 14, 1864, General Banks had testified as
follows regarding General Franklin's movement:

My force was placed under command of General Franklin, who was an officer of high rank, and, as I supposed, of great capacity. I supposed him to
be perfectly capable for the organization of his force of 15,000 men, and
the march up the Red River to Alexandria . . . He was to move on the 5th
of March, and be at Alexandria on the 15th or 17th, where we were to
meet General Sherman.

He [General Franklin] failed altogether to get his troops ready for the
movement at the time. He was not ready to move until the 13th of March.
A severe storm and other difficulties were assigned as the reason for that delay. Moving on the 13th, he reached Alexandria on the 26th of March.[34]

More important than the questions these passages raise—namely, which general's memory was failing him, and was Banks attempting to shift blame to Franklin?—was the fact that the Bobbin Boy had not used the discretion General-in-Chief Halleck had given him, back on February 1, to substitute another course of action if the water level of the Red River did not rise.

As a result, by early March 1864 the Red River was a long magnet attracting warriors and warships to its looping course from its junction with the Mississippi upstream to Alexandria and northwestward to Shreveport. For the better part of a year the rebels' waterway had been the subject of discussions, planning, and sometimes arguments; yet it had remained a wavy line on maps to most of the men who were destined to fight there.

With the coming of spring, though, all that would change. From mid-March onward each day would be marked by action—some on land, much of it on the river, some of it in damp sand. And at the end, fortune was most likely to favor those who gave the most thought to the ways in which water could shape the outcome.

Richard Taylor had made his troop dispositions in anticipation of federal forces' convergence on Alexandria. The elements commanded by Nathaniel Banks and David Dixon Porter were the next to move.

Regardless of whether William Franklin was a competent officer—in December of the next year Banks would imply that he was not—the first man in West Point's class of 1843 (in which U. S. Grant was twenty-first and Frederick Steele was thirtieth of thirty-nine) got his troops moving belatedly, only to be delayed by heavy rains. Franklin was no stranger to the Committee on the Conduct of the War, which had investigated his handling of one phase of the Union's disaster in mid-December 1862 at Fredericksburg—hence his banishment to the Department of the Gulf dumping ground, where he first distinguished himself by getting mauled at Sabine Pass by fifty-odd Texans commanded by a saloonkeeper.[35]

Brigadier General Albert L. Lee's five thousand cavalrymen rode northward before Franklin's infantry moved out and they ran into retarding rains on the day after their departure. Not until March 13, after a week en route, did they reach the town of Franklin, the first waypoint on their ride toward Alexandria.[36]

Lee, born in New York, had been a lawyer in Kansas before the war. Although he had no military training or experience he was commissioned as a major in the 7th Kansas Cavalry and saw action in western Missouri. After brief service during Grant's siege of Vicksburg, in which he was wounded, he was assigned to the Department of the Gulf.[37]

On March 10, while Lee's men were riding through the mud, the ten thousand troops Sherman was loaning General Banks were loading onto twenty-one transports at Vicksburg for the trip down the Mississippi River to the mouth of the Red River, with Alexandria their ultimate destination. In command of this force was Brigadier General Andrew Jackson Smith, a West Point graduate and twenty-six-year veteran of the "Old Army" in the west. Grant and Sherman considered him one of their best officers.

A. J. Smith began sending some of his troops ashore at Simmesport near the Red River's mouth late on the afternoon of March 12. The men celebrated their arrival in Louisiana by burning a house and stealing hogs and chickens.[38]

All of Smith's men were on the road to Marksville on March 14, with Fort De Russy their objective. Confederate General Kirby Smith had ordered De Russy held; Dick Taylor, however, had told General Walker to delay Smith but to avoid a major fight. Walker, with only three thousand men and twelve guns, could hardly be expected to hold back the fifteen thousand to seventeen thousand Yankees rumored to be coming their way with thirty to forty guns.

Someone had overestimated the size of the federal force but it was formidable enough. On that Monday Rear Admiral Porter's gunboats bombarded the three hundred rebel defenders while two brigades of Union infantry led by Brigadier General Joseph A. Mower attacked the fort's rear. After a short fight the Confederates surrendered. The next day Mower's brigades boarded transports for the cruise up the Red River to Alexandria, leaving the rest of Smith's units to destroy Fort De Russy.[39]

Apart from confirming Taylor's belief that forts such as De Russy were useless, a view contrary to that of the general commanding the Trans-Mississippi Department, the engagement was hardly more significant than any other skirmish. Taylor had ordered Walker and his other commanders to concentrate west of Alexandria while he supervised the removal of everything of military value from the town. He was the last Confederate to leave when Porter's gunboats and transports arrived the next day, March 15, 1864. Albert Lee's five thousand cavalrymen were five days south of Alexandria and William Franklin's fifteen thousand infantrymen would not reach Alexandria until March 25.[40]

Up in Arkansas, General Steele had put the election of a governor behind him on March 14, while Mower and Porter were attacking Fort De Russy. But he had developed misgivings about beginning the already-delayed advance southwestward to Shreveport. Implementing Lincoln's political program had used up a great deal of time, rains had turned the roads into creeks of mud, food and fodder were known to be scarce along the route, and rebel guerrillas were active. Steele suggested that he merely make a feint toward the Red River. Grant, by then promoted to lieutenant general and general-in-chief, turned that down. "Move your force in full cooperation with General N. P. Banks' attack on Shreveport," he directed. "A mere demonstration will not be sufficient."[41]

Steele received Grant's telegram on March 15. Two days later he sent orders to Brigadier General John M. Thayer at Fort Smith to start the three thousand troops in his "Frontier Division" on a 170-mile march toward Arkadelphia, with April 1 as his planned arrival date.[42] Thayer, Massachusetts born and a Brown University graduate who was a farmer in Nebraska Territory before the war, departed on Saturday, March 19. Steele, with nearly seven thousand men, left Little Rock on Monday. The next afternoon, nine miles out from his starting point, the only professional officer in the federals' Arkansas units was obliged to put his forces on half rations—except for coffee.[43]

Major General Banks reached Alexandria on his headquarters steamer *Black Hawk* on Thursday, March 24, accompanied by cotton speculators. Porter's sailors had been in the town for nine days, however, and they had been busy, indeed: Navy regulations permitted the payment of certain amounts of cash to personnel who seized ships, materiel, or commodities including cotton as prizes of war, and among the first sights the Bobbin Boy beheld as he disembarked was wagonload after wagonload of captured bales passing on the way to ships waiting at the landing. Banks and the cotton-craving civilians who had come up from New Orleans were horrified and infuriated.[44] Later, in testifying before the Joint Congressional Committee on the Conduct of the War, Banks complained:

> The officers of the navy, during the time we were there, were representing from day to day to the officers of the army the amount of prize money they were to receive, which excited a great deal of bad feeling on the part of the army. All the general officers urged me very earnestly to arrest these men, make war upon them on the ground that they were engaged in a business that did not belong to the navy at all.[45]

To cast a veil of legality over their practice, sailors made stencils enabling them to mark the cotton bales "C.S.A." and "U.S.N." Admiral Porter reportedly laughed when he heard that the initials really stood for "Cotton Stealing Association of the U.S. Navy."[46] Banks was painfully frustrated; he had no command authority over Porter and therefore was blocked from ordering him to stop the practice, and he was prevented from complaining too severely by his critical need for the admiral's cooperation in the drive northward to Shreveport. Moreover, he could do nothing to keep Louisianans from burning their cotton lest it be stolen by Yankees.

Adding to General Banks' discomfort was a message from General-in-Chief Grant, received on March 26 but dated March 15. In it, Grant said that if Banks was not in Shreveport by April 30, he was to abandon the campaign and return forthwith to New Orleans. Worse: Sherman's men had to be returned to Cump by the agreed-upon April 15 *even if* their departure caused Banks' campaign to be aborted short of Shreveport.[47] On April 2 Banks replied that "we hope to be in Shreveport by the tenth of April."[48] His forward elements were then in Natchitoches, at least seventy-five miles south of Shreveport. And Banks was still in Alexandria, completing another step toward executing Lincoln's plan for Louisiana's restoration and watching Admiral Porter struggle to get his gunboats and transports over a mile or more of almost dry rock.[49]

Not yet had David Dixon Porter been obliged to prove that he could take his vessels wherever the sand was damp, but when he reached Alexandria it looked as though the pro-Confederate Red River had whipped him. For the first time in nine years there had been no seasonal rise; rainfall had been far below normal in the stream's vast North Texas and Indian Territory watersheds. Ironically, downpours had made advancing almost impossible for Union forces in southern Louisiana and central Arkansas.

Against the advice of a local river pilot, Porter had ordered his largest ironclad, the *Eastport,* up the trickle (formerly, the rapids) first—whereupon she stuck in the chute, delaying the passage of other vessels the admiral wanted to transfer to the upper stretches of the river. By March 31, however, the *Eastport,* twelve other gunboats, and thirty transports were above the obstacle and Porter was wondering if he would ever be able to get them below it again.[50]

Dick Taylor had learned from Stonewall Jackson that the leader of an inferior force is quite often well advised to withdraw before an enemy's hosts, especially if by so doing that general can lure at least an element of the foe's troops onto ground of his own choosing. Even so, Old Jack's disciple despised the idea of falling back. On March 31 he vented some of his anger in a letter to Kirby Smith:

Had I conceived for an instant that such astonishing delay would ensue before re-enforcements reached me I would have fought a battle even against the heavy odds. It would have been better to lose the State after a defeat than to surrender it without a fight. The fairest and richest portion of the

Confederacy is now a waste. Louisiana may well know her destiny. Her children are exiles; her labor system is destroyed. Expecting every hour to receive the promised re-enforcements, I did not feel justified in hazarding a general engagement with my little army. I shall never cease to regret my error.[51]

Taylor was inclined to overstate his case at times, and this was one of them. But information had reached him to the effect that Hydrocephalus at Shreveport had withheld troops from him. Doctor Sol A. Smith, Kirby Smith's chief surgeon and confidant, was believed to have said that Taylor refused reinforcements Kirby Smith had offered.[52] Seldom in any American war had relations between a subordinate and his superior been so acrimonious, and Taylor's overripe prose hardly eased the strain.

About the only increase that had occurred in Taylor's troop strength had been the arrival of Colonel William G. Vincent's small cavalry regiment on March 19. Taylor lost no time in sending Vincent to Henderson's Hill, about twenty miles north of Alexandria, with admonitions to be vigilant. Only two nights later, however, during a heavy rain storm, Vincent's men were surrounded and captured by a Union force consisting of six infantry regiments and a whole cavalry brigade—A. J. Smith's troops, mostly, commanded by Mower.[53]

That humiliating defeat (most of the captives had not fired a single shot) was still fresh in Taylor's mind years afterward when he wrote:

Vincent's pickets found their fires more agreeable than outposts . . . We lost four guns, with their caissons, and two hundred men. Vincent, with the remainder of his command, escaped. In truth, my horse [mounted infantry] was too ill-disciplined for that work.[54]

Having no cavalry, General Taylor would not learn until later how massive the buildup of federal strength at and near Alexandria really was. Banks' infantry, artillery, and cavalry numbered 14,500. A. J. Smith's 10,000 and various support units brought the total to around 30,000. At the time, Taylor had perhaps 7,000 men to oppose Banks. On the river Admiral Porter had sixty ships, including gunboats, tinclads, supply vessels, and transports. Union army units had ninety artillery pieces; Porter's warships added another 210 guns.[55]

At the end of March, and once Porter had enough gunboats and transports above Alexandria's rapids, General Banks began to send elements of his force northward. His first objective was Natchitoches, roughly fifty miles away and about four miles west of the river landing called Grand

Ecore. Albert Lee's cavalry left first, followed by A. J. Smith's men. Nearly all of the federal units were at Natchitoches or Grand Ecore by April 3, when the general commanding arrived on his flagship, the *Black Hawk*.[56]

On the day before, from Alexandria, Banks had written General Halleck that "we hope to be in Shreveport by the 10th of April," and he added:

> *I do not fear concentration of the enemy at that point; my fear is that they may not be willing to meet us there. If not and if my forces are not weakened to too great an extent, I shall pursue the enemy into the interior of Texas for the purpose of destroying his forces.*[57]

When he read Banks' message several days later, Abraham Lincoln remarked: "I am sorry to see this tone of confidence. The next news we shall hear from there will be of defeat."[58]

Such, certainly, was Dick Taylor's intent. Lest the hordes of federals overwhelm his scattered detachments, as soon as Franklin's troops began their northward march Taylor ordered Mouton, Gray, and Polignac to concentrate on the Bayou Boeuf southwest of Alexandria. Also, he urged Tom Green to hurry eastward from the Sabine.[59]

Withdrawing went against Dick Taylor's grain but two years earlier he had seen how the much-missed Jackson had used maneuver and knowledge of the Shenandoah Valley's complex terrain to defeat every federal force then-acting General-in-Chief Abraham Lincoln had thrown at him. In the days and weeks to come it would often seem that Taylor was reacting to Banks' challenges exactly as Old Jack might have. At a minimum, this natural soldier placed far more trust in his own judgment than in that displayed in spasms from Hydrocephalus at Shreveport. More to the point, like Jackson, Dick Taylor never took counsel of his fears and always backed his convictions with action.

CHAPTER 3

THE DREADFUL DIFFERENCE A ROAD MADE

Washington, D.C., The Capitol, March 9, 1865
Joint Congressional Committee on the Conduct of the War
Testimony of Wellington W. Withenbury

Mr. WELLINGTON W. WITHENBURY sworn and examined.
    By Mr. Gooch:

Question: What is your residence and occupation?
Answer: My residence is Cincinnati, Ohio; my occupation, for twenty-
*   five years, has been that of a steamboat-man, principally upon*
*   the Red River, during the navigable season.*
Question: Did you accompany the Red River expedition, under General
*   Banks, in the spring of 1864; if so, in what capacity?*
Answer: On the 16th March 1864, I reported for duty to Admiral Por-
*   ter, and he requested me to report to him from day to day. At*
*   that time the river was so low that none of his gunboats could*
*   get over the falls at Alexandria . . . Some of the very lightest*
*   boats, denominated tin-clads, could have gone over the falls,*
*   but none others.*[1]

Steamboat-man Withenbury told the Committee about having advised
Admiral Porter against sending the USS *Eastport* through the "chute" and
the delay caused by the naval commander's failure to heed that warning,
then he testified regarding cotton dealings he had witnessed in Alexandria
after the federal naval and army units reached the town in mid-March.

Question: Were you a Union man?
Answer: Yes, sir. The week before General Butler took New Orleans I

*was published in a New Orleans paper as a Union man, and a
man dangerous to the confederacy, and the tree was picked out
to hang me on.*[2]

After commenting on General Banks' having reverted to his Lincoln-
imposed political mission by registering Unionists at Alexandria and conducting an election there, Withenbury volunteered this narrative on
another subject:

[At Grand Ecore, Brigadier General Charles P. Stone, Banks' chief of
staff] *came on board* [Banks' headquarters steamer *Black Hawk*] *and
asked me where Pleasant Hill was. He spread a map out before us, but the
words "Pleasant Hill" were not on it. I traced out the different roads from
point to point, and placed my finger on the spot, and said, "Pleasant Hill is
about there." He said, "I think not." I said, "It is there," and showed him
from other maps. I gave him my own maps for his guidance. During that
same day, perhaps, General Stone, in company with General Banks,
asked me how it would do to cross the river at that point* [Grand Ecore]
and go up on the other [east] *side. I said that it would take them about two
days longer to reach Shreveport, but they would have better roads perhaps.
There was an old military road that led from Campti to Fort Towson, but
they would be obliged to go around some lakes if they went that way. They
then decided not to go that way.*

*I then remarked to them: "When you get above Pleasant Hill, on the
road to Mansfield, you will not see the river any more. You will go further
from the river, and not come within striking distance of it until you get to
Shreveport." I pointed out on the map precisely all the roads. I recollect
asking General Stone one question, and the answer I got indicated that I
was asking too many questions, and I gave it up. It was an unimportant
question, however.*[3]

"The most able of the House members of the Committee," wrote historian T. Harry Williams, "was bespectacled, bearded Daniel Gooch of Massachusetts, whose benign, grandfatherly face seemed incongruous in that
fierce company."[4] Like his colleagues on that panel, however, Gooch had
no military or naval experience, and this may explain his failure to press
Withenbury for more details regarding that conference between the river
pilot and the two generals on the *Black Hawk*. In fact, Major General
Banks' decision to send his troops from the Natchitoches-Grand Ecore vicinity toward Shreveport *via* the road to Pleasant Hill and Mansfield may
have been the most critical blunder he made during the entire campaign.

N

Shreveport

Red River

Loggy Bayou

PORTER

Mansfield

Campti

Pleasant Hill

BANKS

Grand Ecore
Natchitoches

Banks Abandons the Red

Withenbury recalled nearly a year later that during that meeting on April 3, 1864, he had "pointed out on the map precisely all the roads." But had he? Testifying under oath, he had also claimed he was a "good Union man." But was he?

Apparently little or no other thought was given to alternate routes. But the matter had to be settled quickly if Banks was to be in Shreveport on the date he had promised: April 10.

Admiral Porter planned to move on upriver to Loggy Bayou, a stream feeding into the Red River about five miles east of Springfield Landing—from which Banks would open the final phase of his drive. To guard the unarmed vessels in his flotilla Porter would carry with him on twenty transports a division of A. J. Smith's troops commanded by Brigadier General T. Kilby Smith. By leaving Grand Ecore on April 7, Porter expected the fleet to reach Loggy Bayou by April 10; thereafter it would operate on the portion of the river above Alexandria to keep the Union forces in Shreveport and beyond supplied. Kilby Smith's unit would return to General Sherman's army with the rest of A. J. Smith's force on or before April 15.[5]

If that much seemed settled, that other question remained: Should Banks' main body take the road leading from Natchitoches first westward to Pleasant Hill and then northward to Mansfield? But as W. W. Withenbury told the committee, a major disadvantage was the route's divergence from the river and—by implication—from the protection the fire from Porter's gunboats could provide. Also, apparently no person in Banks' army gave much thought to the nature of the terrain ahead, whether water would be available along the way, or if there were routes from Natchitoches to Mansfield other than those Withenbury said he had pointed out to Generals Stone and Banks.

Clearly, Mansfield was an attractive intermediate objective. North of the town three roads led to Shreveport. If time were of the essence this fact could be decisive: Banks had about a thousand wagons in his trains and there would be twenty thousand or more men in his force, and he could occupy his objective faster by using all three routes concurrently.

But no one asked, apparently, whether there was a road along the west bank of the Red River. And it would seem that pilot Withenbury volunteered no information on that point.

Reportedly, General Franklin attempted to persuade Banks to send cavalry patrols upriver and possibly elsewhere to scout the road net. No, the general commanding told him, there was no time for that.

True though that may have been, or seemed to be at the time with Shreveport still the better part of a hundred miles away, in rejecting Franklin's suggestion the Bobbin Boy was revealing his naiveté in matters military: Albert Lee had five thousand troopers, and although by then he was already moving up the road toward Pleasant Hill he could easily have detached a hundred or so of his cavalrymen to find out if there was a road on the river's west bank—or alternate routes to Mansfield.

There was no time for cavalry patrolling, Banks told William Franklin, but Banks had spent another day or so on the president's restoration project. Worse, he lingered at Natchitoches long enough to hold a grand review of his troops and to inspect the more than one thousand wagons in his supply trains. Clearly, Banks was not feeling the pressure of deadlines. To his wife he wrote, "The enemy retreats before us and will not fight a battle this side of Shreveport, if then."[6]

And so it was that on April 6 the advance from Grand Ecore to Shreveport finally began. General Banks had scores of miles to cover and only three more days in which to reach his goal. By taking the inland road he was—in his blithe ignorance—entering a region that was scarcely populated, hilly, with dense forests and thickets on either side of what was little better than a trail, and almost devoid of water. And, ironically, two alternate approaches to Mansfield had been available.

Admiral Porter left the next day, and from the *Black Hawk*'s deck as she steamed up the river he saw what a cavalry patrol would have discovered: a good road following the river's west bank. Later, to General Sherman he wrote:

This would have been the route for the army, where they could have traveled without all that immense train, the country supporting them as they proceeded along. The roads are good, wide fields on all sides, a river protecting the right flank of the army, and gunboats in company.[7]

In early April, as Banks and Porter were pausing at Grand Ecore, General Edmund Kirby Smith was receiving reports from Arkansas to the effect that Frederick Steele's federal force was not as large as earlier estimates had suggested. This made the Trans-Mississippi department's commander wonder if some of Dick Taylor's troops ought to be withdrawn from the Mansfield area, where Taylor was gathering units to resist Nathaniel Banks' advance, and sent northeastward to Sterling Price. So Kirby Smith wrote in a letter to Taylor, asking for his subordinate's opinion.[8]

By striking the weaker enemy force with his concentrated units and destroying it, Kirby Smith would have been acting in accordance with military theory. This may have been one reason for his unwillingness to abandon the possibility. Otherwise, it is difficult to understand how he could place so little weight, apparently, on facts such as these:

- Banks' army was closer to Shreveport than Steele's and it was more than twice as large.
- Time and distance would make transfer of forces from Taylor to Price unduly risky.
- Kirby Smith was under no pressure from Price to return the two divisions Hydrocephalus at Shreveport had pulled back from him earlier.

Still racked by indecision, on April 6 General Smith went down to Mansfield to confer with Taylor directly. Nothing much came of that discussion; Taylor had already expressed his belief that Steele would never reach Shreveport, and he saw no reason to reverse it. However, the department commander did agree to release the two small divisions from Arkansas, then in camps south of Shreveport, to Taylor's control.[9]

Actually, Kirby Smith's forces already operating in Arkansas were having no great difficulty in making the march southwestward a miserable one for Fred Steele. Most of the Confederates were mounted. Three of General Price's five cavalry brigades were commanded by Brigadier General John S. Marmaduke, a Missourian who had been educated at Harvard, Yale, and West Point, wounded at Shiloh, and active since then in raids against Yankee strong points in his native state and Arkansas. Marmaduke delayed Steele's column by attacking the front of it with two of his brigades while a third slashed at its rear.[10]

Steele had ordered Thayer, commander of the Union's post at Fort Smith, to meet him with the Frontier Division on April 1 at Arkadelphia. But Thayer was not there; he did not join Steele until April 9. By that time both elements of the federal army had consumed almost all of their rations. And now that he had thirty-six hundred more mouths to feed, Steele was obliged to send detachments out for miles on either side of his route in search of provisions.[11]

On April 6, while Steele was waiting for Thayer, Colonel Richard M. Gano reported to Price with the brigade of Texas cavalry he had led eastward from the Indian Territory. Price also called in the two brigades that had been watching Yankee activities in the Pine Bluff area. Steele still outnumbered the Confederates, but this was hardly an advantage with starvation an increasingly dangerous threat.[12] Moreover, Price's cavalrymen displayed considerable audacity in harassing the Union columns. What more Price could have done with Taylor's troops, had Kirby Smith sent them, would never be clear.

The threat that Kirby Smith might decide to concentrate on destroying Steele first apparently convinced Dick Taylor that he had better smash Banks as soon as an opportunity presented itself. Accordingly, on Thursday, April 7, he alerted Mouton and Walker to the probability that their divisions (then in camps near Mansfield) would soon see combat.[13] That done, he rode three or four miles south of town in search of a place suitable for slaughtering Yankee invaders. In the right kind of terrain, Jackson had taught him by example, a weak force can defeat a much larger one.

At a clearing called Sabine Crossroads, three miles or so south of Mansfield on the road to Pleasant Hill, General Taylor found conditions to his liking. He reconnoitered the area carefully and made his decisions. After returning to Mansfield he sent two messages. One was to Brigadier Generals Thomas J. Churchill and Mosby Parsons, commanders of the two divisions from Arkansas Kirby Smith had been holding at Keatchie (south of Shreveport), to move down to Mansfield.[14] The other was to Brigadier General William R. Boggs, Kirby Smith's chief of staff at Shreveport:

I respectfully ask to know if it accords with the views of the lieutenant-general commanding that I should hazard a general engagement at this point, and request an immediate answer, that I may receive it before daylight tomorrow morning.[15]

General Taylor was not to receive the immediate reply he had requested. Exactly what happened when his message reached the department's headquarters would never be known. But it arrived on April 8, a day Kirby Smith had proclaimed as one to be devoted entirely to fasting and prayer. Few men were as devout as Edmund Kirby Smith in their observance of religious duties, and he may have assumed Taylor would not move against Banks since all Confederate military operations were supposed to be suspended for the day. In any case, the commanding general wrote a long, ambiguous, and confusing letter to Taylor—according to General Boggs, after he had discussed the situation with Sol Smith, who was not an admirer of Taylor—in which Kirby Smith said:

A general engagement now could not be given with our full force. Reenforcements [sic] are moving up—not very large, it is true. If we fall back without a battle you will be thrown out of the best country for supplies. I would compel the enemy to develop his intentions, selecting a position in rear where we can give him battle before he can march on and occupy Shreveport. I will order down now all the armed cavalry from near Marshall [Texas] and forward Pratt's battery from this point with every available man before a battle is fought. Let me know as soon as you are convinced that a general advance is being made and I will come to the front.[16]

✦──✦──✦

Washington, D.C., The Capitol, January 11, 1865
Joint Congressional Committee on the Conduct of the War
Testimony of Brigadier General A. L. Lee

Brigadier General A. L. LEE sworn and examined.
   By the Chairman, Senator Wade:

Question: What is your rank and position in the army?
Answer: I am a brigadier general of volunteers.
Question: Did you serve under General Banks in what is known as the Red River expedition?
Answer: I did.
Question: Will you, in your own way, go on and state whatever you may deem material in connexion with that expedition? If we desire any more particular information we will question you, either while you are making your statement, or after you have completed it.[17]

General Lee described the advance of his cavalry unit to Alexandria and Natchitoches, his assignment to the portion of Banks' army commanded by Major General Franklin, and the engagements in which he participated on April 7 to 9, 1864.[18] Among other things, he told the committee that:

I had with me a train of wagons, in which we carried for my division [about 3,300 men] ten days' rations for my men, three days' forage for my animals, a large supply of ammunition, and some camp and garrison equipage. This train numbered, I should judge, from 320 to 350 wagons.[19]

So convinced were the generals that the march to their goal, Shreveport, would be uneventful, Albert Lee's wagon train was placed right behind his cavalrymen in the advance that began from Grand Ecore on April 6. Behind Lee's wagons came Franklin's infantry, then the rest of the army's trains, and finally A. J. Smith's troops.

Senator Wade then resumed his interrogation.

Question: Will you state, as far as you know, who first originated this expedition, and what were its objects?

Answer: I cannot speak with any knowledge at all that would avail anything in reference to who originated the expedition. As to its objects, the general idea was that we were going to Shreveport, and perhaps to Texas . . . But I do not believe that anybody had any very well-defined impression as to what we were going for. I am very sure the subordinates had not.

Question: Considering the kind of road, the nature of the country, and the long distance you would be from your base, how could you expect to hold Shreveport, even if you should get possession of it?

Answer: I never supposed we could get to Shreveport.

Question: What do you say of the order of march pursued on your expedition, with the cavalry ahead, and two or three miles of wagon train immediately in the rear? In your opinion, as a military man, was that a proper way of advancing into an enemy's country?

Answer: I remonstrated against it in private conversations and in written despatches, until I am very certain that the parties to whom my remonstrances were made, and those around them, began to think I was getting panicky, as they say, and I had to stop it. I could not allow myself, for reasons which you will understand, to represent further or more urgently my sense of its impropriety.

Question: What was the idea entertained by General Banks and others about meeting the enemy before you got to Shreveport?

Answer: I cannot say as far as General Banks was concerned . . . I believe that the theory was pretty well seated in the minds of the commanding officers that we were not to have any fighting until we got to Shreveport . . . I was laughed at for insisting that we would have a fight before we got to Shreveport; but, as I have already stated, I did not dare to insist upon it after a while, because people began to think I was frightened . . .[20]

On Thursday, April 7, the laughing stopped. Lee's men passed through Pleasant Hill unopposed but three miles north of that village they collided with a brigade of Major General Thomas Green's cavalry that had just arrived from Texas. In his testimony Lee described what happened at Wilson's Farm:

N

Shreveport

Red River

Keatchie

Mansfield

Sabine Crossroads

Pleasant Grove

Sabine River

Wilson's Farm

Pleasant Hill

Mansfield and Vicinity

We met the enemy on a little hill. They were mostly cavalry and mounted infantry, but they had dismounted there. We went into action, putting in a brigade at first. The enemy drove that brigade back about a hundred yards. I then put in the other two brigades dismounted and drove the enemy. We lost about seventy-five killed and wounded there; captured about twenty-five prisoners, and the enemy left on the ground about the same number we lost.

During this action, which occupied about an hour and a half, I sent word to General Franklin . . . and suggested to him to move forward a brigade of infantry to my support . . .[21]

At around five o'clock, Lee received Franklin's reply, sent from Pleasant Hill:

The general commanding has received your despatch of 2 P.M. A brigade of infantry went to the front, but the firing having ceased, it was withdrawn. The infantry is all here. The general directs that you proceed to-night as far as possible with your whole train in order to give the infantry room to advance to-morrow.[22]

When Lee stopped for the night he was ten miles north of Pleasant Hill, facing Green's Texans on the other side of a creek. "We bivouacked on the field," Lee told the Congressmen, "and lay in line of battle all night."[23] But Lee still wanted a brigade of infantry, and he sent Colonel John S. Clark, an aide to General Banks, to find Franklin and renew the request:

I wanted the infantry for the reason [Lee testified] that it was necessary to dismount every cavalryman I put in the fight, and of course their horses made a long, loose, irregular train to lead and take about; and cavalrymen are not fit to fight on foot for a great length of time. I also told [Clark] that my greatest annoyance was my train which was there, and which stretched out for a distance of two or three miles, and must be guarded, which took from one-third to one-half of my force.[24]

Major General William Franklin had graduated first in his class at West Point but he displayed appalling obtuseness in handling Lee's plea. Franklin told Clark to tell Lee that he would send several units of Lee's command detached for rear-area duties earlier back to him, that artillery would be up "if wanted" and could be at Mansfield the next day, and that Lee should "Keep your trains well up."[25]

After midnight Albert Lee's discouragement lifted slightly when a courier arrived with a message from Pleasant Hill. "General Franklin," Lee read, "directs me to say that General Banks is here and by his orders a brigade of infantry will move to your support at 3 A.M."[26]

Actually, in overriding Franklin's flat refusal to send any of his infantry northward, Banks had told Brigadier General Thomas E. G. Ransom to send a division or a brigade to Lee. The army commander probably intended for a division to be ordered forward, since brigades were small. Ransom, educated at Norwich as an engineer, wounded in three earlier fights, used his discretion and dispatched a brigade of only twelve hundred men.[27]

Nothing was done, however, about moving Lee's train to the rear. But this was hardly a surprise to him. Because of the thick forest and underbrush bordering both sides of the road there was no room either for parking the wagons or for turning "two or three miles" of them around.

+=====+

With Mouton's division and Walker's nearby and Tom Green's cavalrymen arriving from Texas, many of Mansfield's residents had departed for Shreveport or East Texas. On Thursday, April 7, General Taylor ordered abandoned houses in the town prepared for use as hospitals. He had already sent word to James Major, whose troopers were down toward Pleasant Hill, to delay the Yankees' advance. Green rode southward that morning and was in command when Albert Lee's Union cavalry engaged the Texans at Wilson's Farm. Early on Friday, according to Dick Taylor's instructions, Green was to withdraw—luring the federals up the forest-lined road to the clearing called Sabine Crossroads.[28]

Soon after sunrise on April 8, the divisions led by Jean Jacques Mouton and John Walker reached the clearing. Taylor directed Mouton to place his brigades on the left side of the Mansfield-Pleasant Hill road, with Walker's men on Mouton's right forming the center, astride the road. When the Yankees emerged from the south Tom Green's cavalry would complete the crescent-shaped line by going in on Walker's right.[29]

Those Confederates, nearly eight thousand in all, were in the edge of the woods on the clearing's west, north, and east sides. In its center was a small hill, and on it in a line facing south across the top of it Taylor placed DeBray's regiment of cavalry—the bait for the trap he was building.[30]

By mid-morning Taylor had received no reply, immediate or otherwise, to the message he had sent Boggs the evening before, the one in which he had declared his intention to fight Banks on Friday. With Banks advancing up the narrow road toward Sabine Crossroads against Green's skirmishers, at 9:40 Taylor sent another message to Shreveport. After describing the situation he added: "I consider this as favorable a point to engage [Banks] as any other." Old Jack would have agreed.[31]

"I will fight Banks if he has a million men," Taylor told Polignac. He promised Mouton the honor of striking the first blow when the right moment came.[32] The men shared the general's ebullient mood; for the better part of four weeks many of them had been obliged to retreat, some of then nearly two hundred miles, but now they were facing an opportunity to smite the Yankees *more* than merely hip and thigh.

Colliding with Tom Green's Texans on Thursday had been enough to solidify Albert Lee's conviction that there would be a much bigger fight soon. But no one else seemed to share his concern.

Early on Friday morning, April 8, General Franklin told the army's commander that he planned to take his forces and wagon trains to a place ten miles west of Pleasant Hill and let them spend the day resting from the long march up from Grand Ecore, much of which had been in mud. Banks had no objection. Indeed, clearing the road of Franklin's troops and seven hundred or so wagons would enable A. J. Smith's units to cover the twenty miles then separating them from Banks faster. That scrap at Wilson's Farm had been just another of Taylor's delaying actions, everyone but Albert Lee appeared to believe; the rebels would go on retreating.[33]

And so it seemed early on that Friday morning to the infantrymen in Colonel Frank Emerson's brigade as they and some of Lee's cavalry pushed northward up the road against light and sporadic resistance. Sure signs the Confederates were not likely to fight were the breakfasts they left behind at one point: Rebels *never* abandoned food.

Soon, though, pushing the Confederates toward Mansfield became more costly. A year later, Albert Lee told the members of the Committee on the Conduct of the War:

> I used the infantry, a regiment in line of battle on each side of the road, with cavalry skirmishers in front, my train following behind. We moved forward very slowly, about half a mile an hour. The enemy occupied every hill, and had as strong a force as we had. We had to drive them by shelling them with artillery, and flanking them. At 11:45 A.M. we had advanced about five or six miles, and reached a point within five miles of Mansfield. I then wrote to General Franklin as follows:
> "The enemy have thus far disputed our progress at every favorable position. We suffered in killed and wounded but advanced steadily. Lieutenant

Colonel Webb just killed. Two or three other officers killed and several wounded."[34]

At noon or close to it, Colonel William J. Landram brought another brigade to Lee, who had requested one earlier because Emerson's infantrymen were getting tired. With Landram's men came General Ransom, their division commander, sent by Banks. Albert Lee's testimony continued:

We came on a large open field of perhaps a mile in extent in any direction. The road ran over a hill, which was an admirable position, and I was surprised, as we came out of the woods, to find that the enemy had abandoned it. I deployed a regiment, skirmished up the hill, found no enemy there, and took possession of the hill. We advanced the skirmishers about half a mile further and found the enemy in force. They were there, infantry and artillery, in line of battle.[35]

Up rode General Banks, accompanied by his staff. "I told him," Albert Lee recalled, "that in my opinion we must fall back immediately, or we must be very heavily re-enforced. I said that the enemy must have some fifteen thousand to twenty thousand men there; four times as many as I had."[36]

Earlier on that Friday morning, while visiting Franklin at his troops' resting place, General Banks had decided to ride to the front, but he said he would return if there was no heavy fighting. "There will be no heavy fighting," Franklin assured him.[37]

Banks did not return but a message came from his aide. It read:

The commanding general desires me to say that the enemy are apparently prepared to make a strong stand at this point, and that you had better make arrangements to bring up your infantry, and to pass everything on the road. The general will send again when to move. He thinks you had better send [word] back and push up the trains, as manifestly we shall be able to rest here.[38]

+‹—•—›+

Resting was about all most of Major General Dick Taylor's Louisianans and Texans had been doing since the middle of that Friday morning. Green's men had finished their work of luring the Yankees to Sabine Crossroads; now they could take position on the right end of the crescent-shaped line and wait for the moment when they and the rest of the Con-

TAYLOR

WALKER   MOUTON

GREEN

BANKS

Sabine Crossroads

federate force would charge yelling and firing into the center of the killing ground from three directions.

Richard Taylor was not a patient man, certainly not as patient as his mentor, Jackson, who used to sit motionless, speechless, hour after hour by his disciple's campfire up in Virginia's Shenandoah Valley. On this Friday Taylor sat on a stump for a while, smoking a cigar, then mounted and rode over to talk to Mouton, then Walker. His eyes and nearly eight thousand other pairs stared out at Honeycutt Hill, where the Yankee in command placed a brigade, then another, then some artillery, with cavalry on both flanks.

As the hours passed more federals appeared; infantry, mostly. Curiously, the Union forces had not attacked. But their line was growing more formidable by the hour, and Jackson had always relished situations in which he outnumbered a fragment of the Union army that was beyond the support of friendly forces.

By early Friday afternoon General Taylor had made a few adjustments, adding strength to Mouton who—he had promised—would draw the first blood, and sending more cavalry to Walker's right. For a time the Confederate commander sat on his horse, smoking, one leg over his saddle. He was certain his army was in the right location, certain that the time for battle had come. Mansfield was a place he could not possibly allow Banks to have. And to stop the federals and turn them back, he would have to strike them before they became too numerous.

Since noon Taylor's patience had been stretched. Too much daylight fighting time had already been lost and not much more remained. At a little after four o'clock he decided that if the Yankees were not going to attack, he would.[39]

✦

General Banks had been diligent in sending back for more of Franklin's infantry. But getting past nearly three miles of Albert Lee's wagons had delayed them on the way up a road that was nothing but a tunnel through the forest and underbrush. Banks, eager to smash the rebels out of his way and get to Mansfield and its three roads leading to Shreveport, sent an aide up to give Lee a message: Move immediately on Mansfield.[40]

"I was a little surprised," Lee told the Congressional inquisitors, "and, more than that, I thought there must be some misapprehension; but the staff officer said that was the order." Banks confirmed that he wanted Mansfield seized when the cavalryman rode back to the command post Banks and his staff had established. "I told him," Lee continued, "we could not advance ten minutes without a general engagement, in which we would be most gloriously flogged."[41]

Nathaniel Banks had revealed how little he understood what was happening when, in the message he had sent Franklin, he included the astonishing idea that "manifestly we shall be able to rest here"—*here* being Sabine Crossroads—even though Banks had been gazing at Taylor's entire force drawn up in line of battle for the better part of three hours. Now reality had eluded him again, or so it seemed, for he was displaying the same weakness in decision-making that had led to his humiliating defeats in Virginia.

But Albert Lee's sound counsel, so emphatically expressed, impressed General Banks enough to suspend the order for the time being. And as if to demonstrate that he was capable of taking some action, he sent more couriers southward bearing exhortations to infantry unit commanders to rush up the road past the wagons to the clearing.[42]

"I went back," Lee testified months afterward, "got in front of my line, got off my horse, and lay down on the ground. I lay there for about fifteen minutes, I guess, when there was very brisk picket firing, and the whole line of the enemy advanced on our flanks and on our front."[43]

Actually, what Albert Lee saw coming toward his line on Honeycutt Hill was Brigadier General Jean Jacques Alfred Mouton's division—Polignac's brigade and Gray's, with Major's cavalry moving at the eastern end of the long formation. Federal infantry rushed down the slope to meet them; artillery south of the hilltop blasted the charging Confederates with canister as both sides fired volleys and men began falling.[44]

Mouton was among the first Confederates to be killed. Polignac took his place. His waves of Louisianans and Texans were driven back at first, but shortly before four o'clock Dick Taylor had moved Colonel Horace Randal's brigade from Walker's division over to support Mouton's and now these regiments—led by Tom Green—hit Union General Ransom's infantry on one flank while cavalrymen responded to James Major's cries of "Give the Yankees hell!" by tearing into the other.[45]

These drives sent Lee's and Ransom's troops reeling back down the road toward Pleasant Hill. Soon the rebels captured three artillery pieces and turned their fire on the fugitives, shredding them with their own canister.[46]

Having seen Mouton's assault sweep the Yankees from one side of Honeycutt Hill, Dick Taylor ordered Green's dismounted cavalrymen, Walker's division, and cavalry units on the extreme right to attack the other—to roll up the federals' western flank. Now he had thrown every man he had into the fight.[47]

Union General Ransom's attention had been riveted to the disaster taking place on his right. But as Walker's and Green's Texans came at his ruined line "yelling like infuriated demons" he ordered an Ohio regiment over to his left to check the rebel threat.[48]

A field army's chief of staff normally remained in the rear to coordinate and expedite units' compliance with the orders of the general commanding, but Charles Stone was in the thick of the fighting. When the Ohio regiment's colonel protested the movement Ransom had directed, Stone enforced the order by leading him and his men westward under heavy fire—but in vain, for they discovered that Ransom's left flank no longer existed.[49]

In fact, Ransom's entire command was disintegrating. Regiment after decimated regiment surrendered or ran toward the woods. Emerson, who had brought the first brigade that came to Albert Lee's assistance early on that Friday morning, was wounded. So was the leader of Ransom's other brigade, and then Ransom himself.[50]

As the shattered and stunned remnants of the Union forces neared the edge of the woods at the clearing's southern end, reinforcements came moving up from the wagon-clogged road. Ahead of one of his divisions rode William Franklin—only to have his horse shot from under him and then to be hit in the leg by a rebel's minié ball.[51]

The appalling slaughter the commander of a Massachusetts regiment beheld compelled him to make a gallant attempt to keep his men from fleeing. "Try to think that you are dead and buried," he yelled, "and you will have no fear!"[52]

Gallant, too, was Nathaniel Banks' conduct as his panic-driven troops streamed past him. "Form a line here!" he shouted. "I know you will not desert me!"[53]

But they did, by the hundreds, throwing away their weapons and ammunition, leaving everything they had carried into the fight with them on the ground as they ran for their very lives.[54]

Louisianans in particular, bent on vengeance, tore after Nathaniel Banks' completely and gloriously flogged troops. At last, after all the weeks and miles of giving up ground, of seeing or hearing about the Yankees' wanton destruction of farms and homes, after worrying about the safety of their loved ones caught in the path of the degenerate invaders, Taylor's men experienced the maddening excitement of victory. As they did, units got mixed but it no longer mattered. Now the nigh-helpless bluecoats were doing their dying in the woods, for their only escape route was blocked by miles of Albert Lee's wagons.

Dick Taylor had been right: Sabine Crossroads was the place and this Friday in early April was the time to smite the enemy hip and thigh.

Surely, from Valhalla, Old Jack was looking down and smiling with approval.

While the fighting had been fiercest a messenger arrived from Hydrocephalus at Shreveport and delivered to General Taylor a letter from the general commanding. In it, Edmund Kirby Smith had told Taylor to avoid a general engagement.

"Too late, sir," Taylor said to the courier. "The battle is won."[55]

Well, yes, the Battle of Sabine Crossroads was won, but the fighting would go on until sundown. Taylor and his Louisianans and Texans pursued the Yankees as best they could through the forests south of the clearing. And this part of the battle would be very different: disorganized, man-on-man.

Chaos prevailed along the road. Some teamsters had tried to turn their wagons around, failed, released their horses and mules or shot them, and fled southward. Many a Union soldier tripped over wagon tongues extending perpendicular to the road, only to be killed, wounded, or captured. About the only thing that saved some was the looting of Albert Lee's train by rebels who had seldom seen such abundance.[56]

Brigadier General William H. Emory, responding to one of Franklin's orders, brought up a division. Rather, he tried to. Emory's mission was to form a line and halt Taylor's pursuit. But as the column moved northward the men in it were shocked to see blueclad solders running toward them yelling "Go back! Go back!"—meaning back to Pleasant Hill. As one of Emory's soldiers recalled:

Still thicker and denser came the frightened crowd, rushing past in every possible manner. Men without hats or coats, men without guns or accoutrements, cavalrymen without horses, and artillerymen without cannon, wounded men bleeding and crying at every step, men begrimed with smoke and powder—all in a state of fear and frenzy, while they shouted to our boys not to go forward any further, for they would all be slaughtered.[57]

Emory, conscious of the scarcity of water in the region, formed his blocking position north of the northernmost of the only two creeks between Sabine Crossroads and Pleasant Hill. Soon Tom Green's Texans drove Emory's division south of the stream. There, the federals held.[58]

But it was late in the day. Men on both sides were exhausted. And for a time it seemed that Nathaniel Banks would have a secure line behind which he could regroup his forces and begin a counterattack the next morning, April 9, the day before the day on which—he had told General Halleck, during a moment of euphoria—he hoped to reach Shreveport.

But the shortage of water proved compelling. Wounded men were rending the night air with pitiful cries for it. Before midnight General Banks ordered a withdrawal to Pleasant Hill.[59]

Dick Taylor, long since, had told Tom Green to prepare to continue the attack the next morning, and then he had turned his horse back toward Mansfield. After touring the houses serving now as temporary hospitals for the wounded, he sent a message to General Smith informing him of the victory and told Churchill, who had led the two Arkansas divisions down from Keatchie and had placed them in camps nearby, to prepare two days' rations and march his men southward at three o'clock in the morning.[60]

General Jackson had always regretted the necessity of fighting on the Sabbath, and now his disciple had profaned with bloodshed the day of humiliation and prayer Kirby Smith had proclaimed. But Jackson had believed, some said, that the Lord took a much dimmer view of ever allowing Yankees to go unscourged. On this basis Taylor had a right to be elated. Instead, he was deeply depressed. Later, he wrote:

Sitting by my camp fire to await the movement of Churchill's column, I was saddened by recollection of the many dead, and the pleasure of victory was turned to grief as I counted the fearful cost at which it had been won. Of the Louisianians fallen, most were acquaintances, many had been neighbors and friends; and they were gone.[61]

Of roughly eight thousand men in Taylor's force, about a thousand were casualties—two-thirds of them in Mouton's division. By attacking, they thinned Nathaniel Banks' ranks of about twelve thousand troops by more than twenty-two hundred. Taylor's Louisianans and Texans captured twenty artillery pieces, more than two hundred of Albert Lee's wagons, many stands of Union units' colors, thousands of small arms (which were particularly important because nearly half of Green's men had arrived from Texas without any weapons), and almost a thousand horses and mules.[62]

"My confidence of success," Taylor wrote afterward, "was inspired by accurate knowledge of Federal movements, as well as the character of their commander, General Banks, whose measure had been taken in the Virginia campaigns of 1862 and since . . . The defeat of the Federal army was largely due to the ignorance and arrogance of General Banks, who attributed my long retreat to his wonderful strategy."[63] But Jackson's pupil had also lured the invaders to a field of battle he had selected, and he had launched his assaults at times when his troops outnumbered the Yankees engaged—first at Sabine Crossroads and then at the creek his men took away from Emory.

But Banks had not been able to use all his resources, apart from the fact that he was obliged to fight twenty miles beyond the reach of supporting fire from Admiral Porter's gunboats, even had they been at the point on the Red River nearest to Sabine Crossroads and not upstream almost as far as Shreveport. Miles of Franklin's supply wagons kept A. J. Smith's troops from being available. Most of the artillery pieces Taylor's men captured were embedded among Lee's train and became impediments rather than assets.

True, Dick Taylor and the men he led had won an impressive victory. But stunning Banks and a fraction of his force had not been enough. The task of destroying the Union army remained, and as that memorable Friday turned into Saturday, April 9, Taylor was preparing to complete it.

CHAPTER 4

Self-Inflicted Wounds

Stonewall Jackson held only one council of war, considered it a mistake, and never consulted anyone again. Robert E. Lee listened politely to suggestions offered informally, but he never sought advice; instead, he acted on his own judgment.

Nathaniel Banks had ignored warnings from his subordinates at Strasburg in May 1862, and he got whipped. And on Friday, April 8, 1864, before and during the battle at Sabine Crossroads he had paid attention only belatedly to Albert Lee's calls for infantry support. But that evening, after William Emory's division had established the line south of the creek, General Banks held a council of war.

Did losing another fight with Taylor cause him to resort to this dimly viewed procedure? Was Banks conceding, in effect, that his judgment alone might not be sound enough to meet adversity's increasingly demanding requirements?

Whatever his reasons may have been, General Banks did preside over a meeting that Friday evening with his senior commanders. Before it convened, however, the Union general commanding had sent a message back to General A. J. Smith at Pleasant Hill ordering him to bring his troops up to the line Emory was occupying.[1] Clearly, Banks' intention was to attack the Confederates in the morning and advance through Mansfield to Shreveport. Did anyone, the general commanding wondered, disagree?

William Franklin, present despite the leg wound he had received late that afternoon at Sabine Crossroads amid the panic, said he did not believe Smith could arrive in time. He also pointed out the obvious fact that thousands of men, among them many who were wounded, were suffering because the rebels had recaptured the creekline—the only water source for miles around.[2]

William Dwight was far inferior to Franklin in rank but he was a close personal friend of Banks and was believed to have more influence over him than anyone. Retreat, and promptly, Dwight counseled, even though the rear was clogged with tired men who had gotten there seemingly on wings of fear. Dwight agreed that Smith was not likely to reach Emory's line by daylight. Lee's cavalry, he noted, was shot to pieces.[3]

"By God, sir, I will not retreat!" Banks had declared to a brigade commander at Strasburg, up in Virginia's Shenandoah Valley, on the night Jackson had been about to block his only feasible escape route, adding: "We have more to fear, sir, from our friends than the bayonets of our enemies!"[4] But on this Friday evening the general may have remembered something else his subordinate had stressed: the difference between a forced retreat and an intentional, planned withdrawal. In any event, Banks ordered his weary army to get on the road to Pleasant Hill forthwith.[5]

Nathaniel Banks was thoroughly experienced in making what are called, euphemistically, retrograde movements. He executed this one with skill despite a road still rendered nigh-impassable by miles of wagons.

Finally, toward morning, Banks' men and A. J. Smith's met, moving at first in opposite directions. *If you live to return,* the veterans of Sabine Crossroads shouted to the newcomers, *you'll travel faster on your way southward again!*[6]

By sunrise Pleasant Hill was being converted into a defensive position, protected for the time being by infantry and artillery blocking the road down which everyone expected Dick Taylor's men to be coming at any moment. Apparently the decision to fortify Pleasant Hill was made by default, for the placement of units was too haphazard to be the work of any single controlling mind. One brigade was lined up at a right angle to the one on its left. Another brigade was completely isolated. Some outfits lacked support on either flank.[7]

Weather may have had something to do with this random deployment, for the day was sunny and warm, the kind of spring day on which no one wants to think about fighting. Fatigue was another factor. Almost all the troops scattered over the plateau had been marching most of the night. Many had worn themselves out earlier, running southward from Sabine Crossroads.

Later, a newspaper reporter described the scene:

General Banks, with his light blue overcoat buttoned closely around his chin, was strolling up and down, occasionally conversing with a member of his staff, or returning the salute of a passing subaltern. Near him was General William B. Franklin . . . His face was very calm that morning, and occasionally he pulled his whiskers nervously . . . General Charles P. Stone, the chief of staff, a quiet, retiring man, who is regarded by the few that know him as one of the finest soldiers of the time, was sitting on a rail smoking cigarettes, and apparently more interested in the puffs of smoke that curled around him than in the noise and bustle that filled the air.[8]

There was a chance, and many men in Banks' army seemed to consider it a strong one, that the rebels would leave them alone on that lazy, comfortable Saturday. Many of Taylor's soldiers had last been seen looting Albert Lee's wagons. And with the road south of Sabine Crossroads cluttered with the wreckage of the cavalry's train, no unit, rebel or federal, had been able to maintain cohesion moving through those dense woods.

Late on that Saturday morning General Banks had gone for a ride to see if anything was happening on the Mansfield road. Finding that nothing much was, he returned to the house he was using for his headquarters and had lunch. Afterward he worked on some messages. To David Dixon Porter, somewhere on the Red River, he had chief of staff Stone prepare a note implying that despite some hard fighting and falling back on Friday, the advance toward Shreveport would be resumed. Wrote Stone to the admiral: "I intend to be in communication with the transports of General Kilby Smith and the gunboats at Springfield Landing on Sunday evening or Monday forenoon."[9]

However, if Banks meant to launch a fresh drive to Shreveport on Sunday morning, why had he—in mid-morning on that Saturday—ordered Franklin's seven-hundred-odd wagons started back toward Grand Ecore?

Nathaniel Banks had been making up his mind and then changing it for most of his military career, but this flaw in his generalship had become increasingly apparent beginning on Thursday, when he had seemed to believe there would be no fighting south of Shreveport. Then on Friday, with Taylor's entire force in plain sight and drawn up in line of battle at the western, northern, and eastern edges of the clearing at Sabine Crossroads, Banks had ordered Albert Lee to attack with Mansfield as his objective— but when warned by the cavalry commander that "We shall be most gloriously flogged," he had backed down. Later on Friday, at Emory's line, Banks called for resumption of the advance on Saturday morning but soon got talked into withdrawing to Pleasant Hill at once, instead. Now, on Saturday afternoon, he was indicating to Porter that he expected to be near Springfield Landing and therefore within striking distance of Shreveport on Sunday or Monday, but at the moment his supply wagons were in fact hours down the road and moving in the *opposite* direction.

In the course of his testimony in 1865 before the Joint Committee on the Conduct of the War, Albert Lee revealed that Banks sent back more than the wagons:

[On Saturday] *morning I was ordered by General Banks to detach one thousand cavalry to act as scouts and skirmishers, and to take the remainder of my division, and take whatever was left of the detachment of the 13th Corps, and some Negro troops that were there, and take the trains and the majority of the artillery of the army to Grand Ecore.*[10]

Why? "It was thought that the enemy would get between us and Grand Ecore," Albert Lee told the Congressional investigators. "[Banks] impressed on me very strongly that, in sending me back from Pleasant Hill, just as the fight was commencing, it was of the greatest importance to save what material we had left."[11]

When Lee said "just as the fight was commencing" he was referring to skirmishing, north of Pleasant Hill, between Confederate and federal cavalry. Another witness testified that the sounds of those clashes grew stronger and nearer as the day wore on.

━━━

For the noise made by the Confederates' approach to have been increasing as the hours of Saturday afternoon passed was a sign that General Richard Taylor might well be in the process of making a major mistake. Perhaps, his mind burdened by many other things, he forgot that Jackson had attacked at "early dawn" whenever he could. And not knowing how General Edmund Kirby Smith would react to his having fought on the day set aside for prayer and fasting, Taylor may have assigned too much urgency to the unfinished task of destroying Banks.

Not wanting to give his enemies any chance to escape, Taylor gave himself the mission of preventing the Union force on the Red River from joining the one led by Banks. Evidently he was not aware of how far upstream Porter's flotilla had steamed. Also, Taylor was overestimating the number of T. Kilby Smith's federals on the transports. In any case, on Friday night he assumed that Banks might have fallen back to Pleasant Hill to gain access to a road leading eastward from there to Blair's Landing, sixteen miles away but the nearest point on the Red River at which Banks and Kilby Smith's waterborne troops could reestablish contact. Accordingly, Taylor had sent cavalry to block the Pleasant Hill-Blair's Landing road.[12]

Uppermost in Taylor's mind, however, was catching up with Banks and crushing him as soon as possible, certainly before the survivors of Sabine Crossroads could reach the Red River itself and Porter's fleet at Grand Ecore. Getting tangled units sorted out took most of the night. Some of Taylor's men spent it rounding-up Yankee mules and horses and driving the captured supply wagons to the rear. Churchill's division and Parsons' were moving southward from their camps near Mansfield. Beyond the creek they had taken away from Emory's federals the men behind Taylor's picket lines (and, no doubt, some in it) got such rest as hard ground and very few hours afforded.[13]

Around sunrise the Confederates discovered that Emory's positions had been abandoned. As Taylor and Tom Green led cavalry toward Pleasant Hill they found the road littered with evidence of the invaders' demoralization: weapons, knapsacks, burning wagons and ambulances, bodies of dead and wounded men and stragglers. Chimneys were all that remained of farm houses the fugitives had burned along the way.[14]

Green's Texans pressed Banks' rear guard vigorously enough to take some prisoners, including New York Zouaves whose gaudy uniforms with baggy pants prompted one cavalryman to suggest that the war must be almost over because Lincoln was having to send women to do his fighting. But resistance stiffened as the skirmishing neared the little village. That was all right with Taylor, at least for the time being, for he did not want to bring on a general engagement until all of his forces were up and in position for a devastating attack.[15]

By nine o'clock on Saturday morning Taylor was probing Banks' lines with light cavalry attacks. He also did some scouting, riding past ravines and through stands of trees, noting the locations of Union army units, figuring out how best he could employ the divisions led by Churchill and Parsons. Mouton's depleted division, now Polignac's, he would have to keep in reserve. But Tom Green's men and Walker's were up, bringing with them some of the artillery captured the day before at Sabine Crossroads.

Dick Taylor's plan of attack called for the two divisions from Arkansas to make a Jacksonian wide envelopment of Banks' line, striking it from its western flank and rear as Green and Walker assaulted the federal center and cavalry closed in from the east—and also blocked the Blair's Landing road in case Banks tried to use it as an escape route.[16] True, the men in Churchill's and Parsons' divisions, roughly four thousand in all, had done no fighting and therefore were considered "fresh"; but when they began arriving, early on that Saturday afternoon, it was clear that they were completely worn out:

> They had marched forty-five miles [Taylor wrote later], and were thoroughly jaded. Walker's and Polignac's divisions had been heavily engaged on the previous day, and all were suffering from heat and thirst. Accordingly, two hours were given to the troops to lie down and rest.[17]

Admirable though Dick Taylor's compassion may have been, it delayed

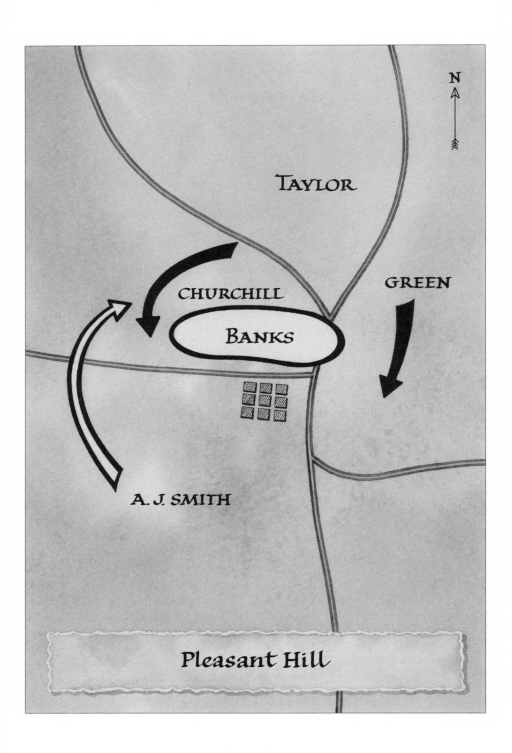

N

TAYLOR

GREEN

CHURCHILL

BANKS

A. J. SMITH

Pleasant Hill

the start of Churchill's and Parsons' movement until after three o'clock. At this point in the day Taylor might have decided to wait until early dawn on Sunday to launch his assault. But he was not as patient as Jackson, at least on this occasion, and he sent the maneuvering force westward though he must have known the shadows would be getting very long before those units got around and behind Banks' lines.

✦

Time remaining on that Saturday afternoon for fighting was severely limited; even more so was the amount of information General Taylor had been able to give Churchill regarding the terrain, roads, and federal troop dispositions in and around Pleasant Hill. The town consisted of a few houses, a store or two, and a school building locally referred to as the college. At its northern edge the Sabine River road from the northwest met the north-south road connecting Mansfield and Grand Ecore. From vantage points roughly a mile north of the village it appeared that Banks' forces were scattered in a manner meant to prevent the Confederates from approaching on either road. More difficult to discern, however, were the western and eastern ends of the Union army's ragged formation. Also, ravines and clumps of trees between the federal lines and Taylor's units added complexity to the task of preparing for battle.[18]

Afterward, Taylor described the mission he had assigned to the enveloping element's commander:

> Churchill, with two batteries and three regiments of horse [mounted infantry] was directed to move to the right [west] and turn the enemy's left [flank]. His route was through the forest for two miles to the road coming from the Sabine. The enemy's left outflanked, he was to attack from the south and west, keeping his regiments of horse well to his right, and Walker would attack on his left. This was explained to Churchill, and Mr. T. J. Williams, formerly sheriff of De Soto parish, and acquainted with every road in the vicinity, was sent with him as a guide.[19]

When Churchill reached "the road coming from the Sabine" he placed Brigadier General Mosby M. Parsons' division on the southwest side of it and his own brigades, now led by Brigadier General James C. Tappan, on the northeast. Their advance, however, took them toward the center of Banks' line, not its western flank and definitely not its rear; discovering this, Churchill shifted his troops to place more of them west of the road. Even then Yankees were on his right flank. And by that time Tappan's troops were starting a spirited firefight with a federal brigade commanded by Brigadier General Lewis Benedict, whose position in Banks' defenses was well east of the line's western end.[20] As Taylor recalled this clash:

> *The attack ordered, the Missourians threw themselves on the enemy, drove him from the gully and the thicket, mounted the plateau, broke an opposing line, captured and sent to the rear three hundred prisoners, got possession of two batteries, the horses of which had been killed, and reached the village.*[21]

When sounds of the firing reached the men in Walker's division they attacked straight ahead, plunging into William Shaw's brigade, which was also getting hit from the east by James Major's cavalry. Tom Green sent regiments of Texan troopers commanded by Brigadier General Hamilton Bee and Colonels August Buchel and Xavier De Bray charging down the Mansfield-Pleasant Hill road. But Shaw's federals caught them in a deadly crossfire, emptying many saddles including those of Buchel and De Bray.[22]

Xavier De Bray, pinned under his horse, finally got free by working his leg out of a boot. Using his sword for a cane, he limped to Dick Taylor's command post. "I was sent on a bootless errand," he quipped. And Taylor replied: "Never mind your boot, you have won your spurs."[23]

Not so lucky was the gallant German-Texan, August Buchel. Striking at Shaw's main line he was mortally wounded and died within a few hours, with General Taylor was at his side.[24]

Although the Yankees seemed to be taking catastrophic losses and reeling back toward the village everywhere the Confederates were assaulting, a critical factor had either been overlooked or obscured and masked by buildings, the terrain, and battlesmoke: the presence of A. J. Smith's troops, which had not been engaged earlier because in the somnolent portion of the day General Banks had designated them as his reserve. Smith's men had watched Churchill make the mistake of not going far enough westward in his advance to get around and behind *all* of Banks' forces. And Smith's fresh troops, most if not all of them entering combat for the first time during this campaign, punished those led by the former Little Rock postmaster for his lapse by launching a counterattack that—combined with fast-increasing darkness—caused Dick Taylor to withdraw his units northward, leaving Nathaniel Banks in possession of acres of battlefield littered with dead and wounded men.[25]

To the extent that Banks could claim Pleasant Hill as a victory, he owed a tremendous debt to Benedict, killed in action while blunting Churchill's drive, and to Shaw, and most of all to A. J. Smith. As the night spread over a scene resembling hell itself, Banks found Smith. "God bless you, General," he said, shaking Smith's hand. "You have saved this army."[26]

A. J. Smith's understanding was that General Banks meant to attack northward early the next morning, Sunday, April 10. Smith was also aware that Banks had sent a courier down the road to Grand Ecore to tell Albert Lee to turn the seven-hundred-odd supply wagons around and bring them back to Pleasant Hill. It came as a shock, then, when later on Saturday evening A. J. learned that the army commander had held another council of war at which Franklin and Dwight had *again* persuaded him to retreat— this time, all the way back to Grand Ecore.[27]

In the Committee on the Conduct of the War's hearing room in the Capitol's basement on January 6, 1865, Chairman Ben Wade professed shock, also, and asked General Franklin:

> Question: *What do you, as a military man, say about retreating from [Pleasant Hill]? Or do you think it should have been held?*
>
> Answer: *In the first place, the cavalry had all been sent back to the rear that morning, with the exception of about five hundred men. The 13th Corps detachment had also been sent to the rear. The horses that morning had been without food for thirty-six hours. There was nothing for them to eat, and there was nothing for the cavalry men to eat, for their trains had all been captured the day before. There was no water at Pleasant Hill for either men or animals. The enemy's picket line could have kept us from getting any water at any time. I wanted the army to fall back to the river, but at a point only fifteen miles from Pleasant Hill [Blair's Landing]. I knew that there we could reach our transports and protect them. But General Banks preferred going on to Grand Ecore. By falling back to the river we would have been joined by the cavalry, the 13th Corps, and a brigade of General A. J. Smith's command, under Brigadier General Kilby Smith, and we would have had our transports and forage with us.*[28]

But Franklin's proposal had been rejected: Porter was not reported anywhere near Blair's Landing; no one knew where he was. Moreover, the rebels were thought to be blocking the road leading to the river and none of Banks' subordinates at the meeting wanted any more fights with Dick Taylor's forces just then.

Actually, the federal officers had estimated Taylor's troop strength at up to twenty-five thousand when in fact he had attacked the Union's eighteen-thousand-man army with less than twelve and a half thousand. Feeling that they were outnumbered discouraged Banks' advisors, but there was also a massive loss of confidence in Nathaniel Banks. As Franklin testified later: "From what I had seen of General Banks' ability to command in the field, I was certain that an operation dependent on upon plenty of troops, rather than upon skill in handling them, was the only one which would have probability of success in his hands."[29]

Unable to believe the report that Banks had changed his mind and had ordered a retreat, A. J. Smith found him and delivered an angry protest. Give me time, Smith requested in effect, to bury my dead—at least to collect my wounded. He was also worried about freeing Taylor to block the river and trap the transports carrying Kilby Smith's men far beyond the reach of rescue forces. But Banks was, for once, adamant. He refused to allow Smith to remain at Pleasant Hill until noon on Sunday, or even until nine o'clock the next morning.

Appalled, Smith found Franklin and urged him, as second in command, to place Banks under arrest. After thinking it over, Franklin replied, "Smith, don't you know this is mutiny?"[30]

Smith had a right to be bitter about more than converting a tactical victory into a strategic defeat, as well as having to leave his wounded behind and his dead unburied. Of all the Union generals on the field that Saturday, he was the only one who had made a decision: the one to counterattack.

Banks had been present, but that was all. He had allowed the army to dispose itself in a manner that can charitably be called *weird*. And he had exercised absolutely no influence on the conduct of the battle.

Yet, had he *not* been inert, the results for the Union might have been worse. As it was, the federals lost nearly fourteen hundred men—more than nine hundred of them in Benedict's and Shaw's brigades. Confederate casualties amounted to roughly sixteen hundred.[31]

More than any other Union officer, Albert Lee ought to have been thoroughly accustomed to General Banks' habit of changing his mind. Even so, the cavalryman was surprised into disbelief when a courier arrived with orders to return to Pleasant Hill. Lee had already sent an aide northward to find out what was going on when one of Banks' staff officers came riding up. Now Lee was directed (he testified) "to continue pressing on with the whole train to Grand Ecore, and if any wagons broke down to burn them, not stop to fix anything, but get everything to Grand Ecore as quickly as I could, and look out very carefully on the flanks."[32]

Success is a Duty, Banks had maintained from his days as a bobbin boy in a Waltham, Massachusetts, textile mill to this night at Pleasant Hill, Louisiana, and his fidelity to his motto was reflected in his report on the battle:

The defeat of the enemy was complete, and his loss in officers and men more than double that sustained by our forces . . . The enemy was driven from the field. It was as clear a rout as it was possible for an army to suffer.[33]

Curiously, Richard Taylor was not conscious of having been routed. Darkness caused him to order Polignac's and Green's troops disengaged, and he moved all his units but Bee's cavalry back five miles toward Mansfield so that his men could have access to water. Confident that surgeons and others were taking care of both sides' wounded at Pleasant Hill, Taylor found a spot about two hundred yards from the battlefield and, as he put it, "threw myself upon the ground."[34]

Earlier that evening Taylor had tried to ease Churchill's depression. He summarized his own feelings years later by calling the results of the Confederate effort at Pleasant Hill "creditable," adding:

Yet [they were] of much less importance than those that would have been accomplished but for my blunder . . . Instead of intrusting the attack by my right to a subordinate, I should have conducted it myself and taken Polignac's division to sustain it . . . I was confident that the enemy had no intention of resuming the offensive, and should have acted upon that conviction. All this flashed upon me the instant I learned of the disorder of my right. Herein lies the vast difference between genius and commonplace: one anticipates errors, the other discovers them too late.[35]

Richard Taylor's sleep was interrupted, not long after he threw himself on the ground, by the arrival from Shreveport of General Edmund Kirby Smith, commander of the Confederacy's Trans-Mississippi Department. Smith's sixty-five-mile ride had started on Saturday morning when he had received the message Taylor had sent the night before, the one reporting his victory at Sabine Crossroads. Now there was another battle for Taylor to admit he had fought without orders or permission.

Unable to offer hospitality of his own, Taylor took his visitor to Hamilton Bee's nearby campfire where coffee was to be had. Bee's cavalry was far south of there, led by De Bray, pursuing Banks' retreating forces. The host at the campfire informed both of his superior officers that the infantry had gone to Carroll's Mill, one of the string of supply depots Dick

General Edmund Kirby Smith, CSA

Taylor had established between the Bayou Teche region in southern Louisiana and Mansfield, using loot captured from the Yankees in the 1863 fighting west of New Orleans. Most of the cavalry not then chasing Banks, Bee said, was refitting in Mansfield.[36]

Hamilton Bee, Kirby Smith and Taylor would recall, was the older brother of Barnard Bee, killed at First Manassas in July 1861, but remembered as the man who had given Jackson the nickname Stonewall. Though born in South Carolina, both Bee brothers had later adopted Texas as their home.[37]

Once Kirby Smith had been briefed, he and Taylor rode up to Mansfield. There, on Sunday, April 10, the amiability of their campfire talks would degenerate into politely expressed acrimony.[38] But it would be a while before they discovered how profoundly certain events on the Red River and in Arkansas that Sunday and the day following it would affect their decisions and actions for the rest of the Red River campaign.

First, Loggy Bayou.

This was the point on the Red River at or near which the rendezvous of Admiral David Dixon Porter's flotilla and General Nathaniel Banks' army (less sixteen hundred federals under T. Kilby Smith afloat on transports) was to take place. Springfield Landing was another name for Porter's and Banks' objective, though it was located on an old loop of the river a few miles to the west. Both places were roughly thirty miles south of Shreveport and, according to plans made nearly a week earlier at Grand Ecore, would be the launching sites for Banks' drive into the town thought to be the gateway to East Texas.[39]

The flotilla had reached Loggy Bayou in a little more than three days, but for Admiral Porter the hundred miles of coping with wretched conditions on the pro-Confederate river had been agonizing. Getting his temporary flagship, the tinclad gunboat *Cricket*, upriver would have been challenging enough, given low water, hidden snags and stumps on the bottom, and a treacherous and narrow channel. But with *Cricket* came the powerful river monitors *Osage* and *Neosho*, the *Fort Hindman* (another tinclad), the armed steamer *Chillicothe*, the naval transport *Benefit*, tugboats *Dahlia* and *Brown*, and the *Lexington*, a wooden gunboat. Also in Porter's flotilla were more than twenty transports and supply boats. And when any vessel ran aground, as did the transport *Iberville* on the second day, the entire fleet was obliged to wait until all could proceed.[40]

Confederate scouts on the western bank's bluffs kept up with the Union force but did not molest it. Their presence, however, suggested that getting downriver might be much more difficult than steaming up it if Nathaniel Banks' column had not shattered Taylor's forces at some point.[41]

About a mile above Loggy Bayou Porter's course was blocked by a steamboat, the *New Falls City*, the Confederates had placed with about fifteen feet of her bow embedded in one bank and her stern in the other. "It was," Porter wrote General Sherman, "the smartest thing I ever knew the rebels to do," adding that attached to the ship's side was an invitation to attend a ball in Shreveport.[42]

Kilby Smith sent a party ashore on the west bank to hunt for Banks' troops. Soon afterward, though, as the federals were looting farm houses between Loggy Bayou and Springfield Landing, a Union army captain leading fifty cavalrymen arrived with word for Porter that Banks had been defeated at Sabine Crossroads on Friday, April 8, two days earlier, and had fought again at Pleasant Hill twenty miles south of there on Saturday. The bearer of the disturbing news also had a verbal order for Kilby Smith from General Banks: turn back.

Porter recognized at once that the sooner he got his fleet well down the river, the better his chances would be of saving his ships and Kilby Smith's men and supplies from being blown out of the damp sand by Dick Taylor's artillery. Even without vexation from the river's banks, however, turning more than thirty steamboats around in a narrow channel would take much time; also, frequent accidents would be inevitable, the only questions being *when* they would occur and *how damaging* they would prove.[43]

The other event on April 10, 1864, bearing on the heated discussions Generals Edmund Kirby Smith and Richard Taylor were having at Mansfield, was a meeting engagement on the Prairie d'Ane, about fifteen miles southeast of Washington, Arkansas. For the first time in the campaign the armies of Frederick Steele and Sterling Price, each reinforced within the past few days, were in contact. The fighting that day built into skirmishing punctuated by artillery exchanges and it settled nothing—or so it seemed.[44]

On the day before, Saturday, April 9, while Dick Taylor's forces were preparing to attack Banks' oddly deployed troops at Pleasant Hill, Brigadier General John Thayer's thirty-six-hundred-man Frontier Division had reached Frederick Steele's army. The contingent from Fort Smith, which brought along as an artillery battery's mascot a tame bear named Postlewait, was more than a week late and it had consumed all of its rations on the way. Steele had nothing to give them, for during the wait for Thayer his soldiers had eaten almost all the provisions that were supposed to last them until they arrived at Shreveport.

The federal major general commanding sent a courier back to Little Rock with an urgent order for thirty days' rations for fifteen thousand men, a sign that he meant to press on. But now he faced Sterling Price's entire force, including troops from the Indian Territory and detachments of cavalry that had been guarding against a Union threat from east of Camden.[45]

Soon, then, Fred Steele would have to decide whether to attack Price in the hope of reaching Shreveport before starvation thinned his ranks, or to hold on the Prairie d'Ane to wait for rations that might or might not be forthcoming from Little Rock, or to concede that he could not accomplish his mission and retreat to his starting point. And, apparently, Steele would have to make up his mind without any information at all from General Banks and Admiral Porter.

At various times Edmund Kirby Smith had thought seriously of entering the Episcopal ministry.[46] Having to deal with a soul as restless, impatient, often arrogant as Dick Taylor's surely must have made the Trans-Mississippi Department's commanding general wish he had answered The Call. But, fittingly, charity and fellowship prevailed for a time on Sunday, April 10. Kirby Smith assured Taylor of his admiration and support, and Taylor asked his superior to pardon his heathenish ways.

But the hatchet did not long remained buried. Kirby Smith expressed the belief that further pursuit of Nathaniel P. Banks was not as important as protecting Shreveport from attack by Frederick Steele's federal column, then said to be about 110 miles away and approaching Washington, Arkansas, from the northeast. Moreover, the senior general was concerned lest Banks' troops leave their transports at Loggy Bottom and block communication between Shreveport, Mansfield, and points south.[47]

Taylor thought that possibility most unlikely, much as he may secretly have wished for isolation from Hydrocephalus at Shreveport. And as was characteristic, he risked relief for insubordination (once more) by advocating the concentration of all forces in Louisiana and their solemn dedication to the destruction of Nathaniel Banks' army and the capture of all the gunboats and other vessels in David Dixon Porter's highly vulnerable flotilla. Steele and Porter would both rush back to their bases, Taylor predicted, as soon as they learned that Banks was bound not for Shreveport but for Grand Ecore and maybe even New Orleans.[48]

Yet General Banks' flight from Pleasant Hill suggested to Kirby Smith that those Yankees no longer constituted a threat to Shreveport and that, therefore, the bulk of Taylor's troops ought to be recommitted at once to

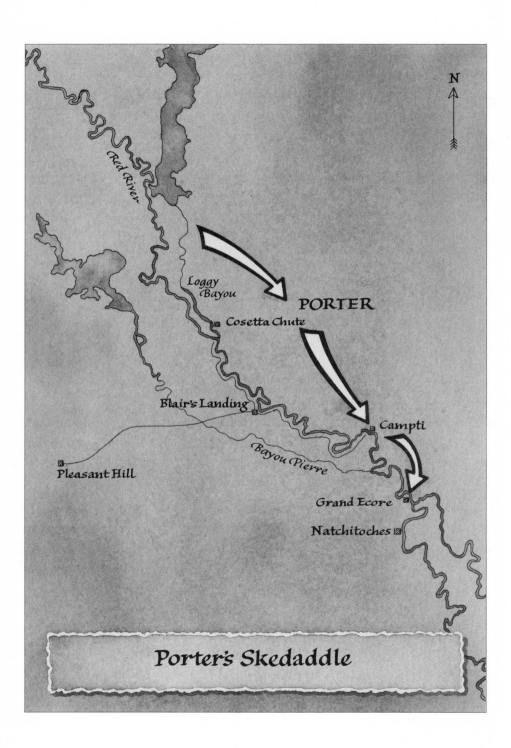

N

Red River

Loggy
Bayou

Cosetta Chute

PORTER

Blair's Landing

Campti

Bayou Pierre

Pleasant Hill

Grand Ecore

Natchitoches

Porter's Skedaddle

the destruction of Steele in Arkansas.[49] In theory, he was correct. And it was not clear that Price had enough men to annihilate Steele's ten-thousand-odd.

But turning away from Banks, Taylor maintained, made no sense:

> Banks [he wrote afterward], with the remains of his beaten army, was before us, and the fleet of Porter, with barely enough water to float upon. We had but to strike vigorously to destroy both. But it was written that the sacrifices of my little army should be wasted, and, on the morning of the 10th, I was ordered to take all the infantry and most of the horse to Mansfield.[50]

Kirby Smith returned to Shreveport that day. But Taylor could not abide letting Banks escape, especially in view of the lives lost in stopping him at Sabine Crossroads and Pleasant Hill. He said so in a lengthy message that brought the general commanding back to Mansfield on Wednesday, April 13. Again Kirby Smith rejected Taylor's arguments. And again Taylor refused to cease offering them; on Friday, April 15, he rode to Shreveport to present them one more time.

By then Kirby Smith had received word from Sterling Price that Steele had turned away from the road to Shreveport and was heading for Camden. That news convinced Taylor that troops sent to Price would be marching a hundred miles or more on a bootless errand. But the department commander reiterated his intention not only to reinforce Price, but to take Taylor's infantry up there and to assume command of the combined force when he arrived.

Taylor's services in this operation, Kirby Smith informed him, were not desired. Instead, he was to remain in nominal charge of the headquarters at Shreveport. But Taylor could, if he wished, go southward and keep an eye on Banks. Having just implied that he did not put much weight on where Taylor went or what he did, Kirby Smith then told him that he was promoting him to the rank of lieutenant general.[51]

And so it was that Edmund Kirby Smith marched northward with all of Taylor's infantry except Polignac's remnant of a division, determined to catch an enemy already retreating and bring him to battle. Was this a serious reflection of his military judgment? Or was it a desperate attempt to salvage something of his reputation, a childish response, evidence of his jealousy of Taylor's success at Sabine Crossroads?

Strange indeed and nigh inexplicable, Richard Taylor may well have joined A. J. Smith in thinking, are the ways of commanding generals.

Rear Admiral David Dixon Porter, USN

General Taylor had not waited until his differences with the Trans-Mississippi Department's commander were settled to send cavalry to two points on the Red River's west bank with orders to capture or destroy Admiral Porter's gunboats and transports. The guns at Pleasant Hill had barely cooled when he ordered Brigadier General Arthur P. Bagby to take his brigade to Grand Bayou, upstream from Blair's Landing. And if the Yankee flotilla got past Bagby, Taylor knew he could count on Tom Green and his troopers to trap it at Blair's Landing.

For once terrain and weather favored the invaders. Bayou Pierre, a rain-swollen stream both Confederate detachments had to cross, caused delays that enabled Porter's fleet to get below Bagby's destination. Another factor was the refusal, earlier, of Hydrocephalus in Shreveport to pay any heed at all to Dick Taylor's repeated requests for permission to use a pontoon train parked at department headquarters, where this vital bridging equipment was utterly useless. Green, as well as Bagby, lost precious time for the same reasons.[52]

At the outset of David Dixon Porter's attempt to steam to safety at Grand Ecore the river seemed to be his (more to the point, his vessels' captains') most distressing adversary. On the first day a submerged stump held the *Chillicothe* prisoner for several hours until a tow line from the *Black Hawk* pulled her off. On Monday, April 11, it was the transport *Iberville's* turn to idle the other thirty-odd craft in Porter's fleet by running aground. Other boats got into trouble. As delays lengthened Confederates on the west bank's bluffs began firing minié balls at every Yankee unwise enough to try to free them. Finally, toward dark the transport *Emerald* ran aground.[53]

Although Kilby Smith had mounted artillery on the decks of the steamers carrying his men, few souls aboard them were brave enough to leave the shelter of barricades formed by cotton bales and go out to serve the pieces. But the navy's gunboats responded with eleven-inch rounds, a remedy that inspired more awe than fear. Night halted the firing and cloaked the federals' efforts to get all the vessels in the flotilla ready to move southward early the next morning, Tuesday, April 12.[54]

That day's adventures were recorded in the veteran wooden gunboat *Lexington's* log:

> At 9 A.M. *collided with the* Rob Roy, *staving wheelhouse and launch and damaging chimneys. Lay to, to repair damages. At 2 P.M. stood down river. At 2:50 were fired on from shore; threw a couple of shell. At 3:15 boats in rear gave five whistles; sent the* Brown *back to assist them if neces-*

sary. At 4:30 P.M. overhauled the transports tied up to the bank—the Alice Vivian aground, the Osage lying below her. At 5:40 the enemy, 1,500 strong, with 2 fieldpieces, attacked the Vivian and transports near her from the right bank . . . [55]

Lieutenant George M. Bache, commander of the Lexington, described the Confederate attack in a report to Admiral Porter:

I have the honor to report that yesterday afternoon the enemy opened on the rear end of the fleet with three pieces of artillery, the Osage and this vessel being the only gunboats present. I immediately got the Lexington under way, steamed past all the other vessels toward the battery, engaged it with our bow guns (VIII-inch) and drove it off in a few minutes, disabling one of the pieces. When within 600 yards of the battery, we encountered a very heavy fire of musketry from some fifteen hundred men, whom we passed at a distance of twenty feet. The enemy came boldly up to the edge of the bank, yelling and waving their side arms, so close that as a portion of the bank caved in from our fire, one of the rebels tumbled down within a few feet of the vessel. I now got our port bow broadside to bear on the enemy's line, and while the Osage poured in a front fire of grape and canister, we raked them with shell and shrapnel. They retreated precipitately into the woods after an engagement of forty minutes, having experienced a loss in killed and wounded of about 150 men, among them General Green, their commander and one of their colonels.[56]

Admiral Porter provided additional details, some of which differed from other accounts, in a letter written on May 4 to A. J. Smith. Porter placed Green's strength at twenty-five hundred backed by another five thousand. Confederate casualties other than Green, "their best general," said Porter, were "about twenty officers and four or five hundred men."[57]

Lieutenant Commander Thomas O. Selfridge, of the Osage, put the rebel loss at "not less than two hundred." In his report he said that the Confederates delivered "the heaviest and most concentrated fire of musketry that I have ever witnessed."[58]

Richard Taylor, writing years afterward, made this wry comment on the variations in numbers:

The enemy's loss, supposed by our people to have been immense, was officially reported as seven on the gunboats and fifty on the transports. Per contra, the enemy believed that our loss was stupendous; whereas we had scarcely a casualty except for the death of General Green, an irreparable

*one. No Confederate went aboard the fleet and no Federal came ashore; so
there was a fine field of slaughter in which the imagination could disport itself.*[59]

But for all of Green's gallantry and that of his men, the Yankee flotilla
steamed on past Blair's Landing. On the next day, Wednesday, April 13,
accidents continued to plague David Dixon Porter's fleet. *Rob Roy* had to
be towed because of a broken rudder. The transport *John Warner* ran
aground and stayed there. Confederate Brigadier General St. John R.
Liddell placed artillery fire on the flotilla from the river's east bank, but the
Osage's eleven-inch guns drove the rebels away.[60]

Late on Monday night the last men in General Banks' rear guard arrived
at Grand Ecore, ending the two-day, forty-five-mile retreat. But no word
from Admiral Porter was waiting there, and when sounds of gunfire
reached Grand Ecore on that Wednesday no one knew what was happening upriver.[61]

Colonel William Shaw guessed that Porter and Kilby Smith might be in
trouble and asked the army commander for permission to take his brigade
over the pontoon bridge to the river's east bank and up toward Campti,
where the action appeared to be. Banks refused; Shaw went to A. J. Smith,
who agreed that the Bobbin Boy was sadly deficient in military ability.
Smith regretted his own lack of authority to bless the venture. Shaw led his
men over the bridge and up the road anyway.

Meanwhile, Admiral Porter had arrived at Grand Ecore and pointed out
to General Banks that the boats stranded up at Campti needed infantry
protection. Banks, learning that Shaw had gone ahead, reversed himself
and ordered A. J. Smith to take a brigade and follow him.[62]

But Liddell's threat had long since passed when A. J. Smith and Shaw
and their brigades arrived, and on the next day Kilby Smith ordered the
transports to steam down to Grand Ecore. By Friday, April 15, even the
John Warner and the *Fort Hindman*, the transport's guardian gunboat, were
safe—like all the vessels that had left Loggy Bayou four days before,
scarred, stacks shot full of holes, but safe.[63]

Nathaniel Banks, convinced that Taylor had twenty-five thousand
screaming Confederates who were about to smite him, ordered Grand
Ecore fortified and otherwise prepared to withstand a siege. That done, the
general commanding sat down to write General Sherman an explanation
of why he was not returning on the date agreed upon the ten thousand
troops he had borrowed.

CHAPTER 5

THEY ALL SKEDADDLED TO GRAND ECORE

Seeing the Union army commander at the side of the road as though he were taking a review, the weary men in the ranks sang as they ended the long, rapid march from Pleasant Hill:

> *In eighteen hundred and sixty four,*
> *Foot balls, foot balls;*
> *In eighteen hundred and sixty four,*
> *Foot balls, says I;*
> *In eighteen hundred and sixty four,*
> *We all skedaddled to Grand Ecore*
> *We'll all drink stone blind,*
> *Johnny fill up the bowl!*

And then they shouted, *"Napoleon P. Banks!"*[1]

Aboard his flagship *Cricket*, Admiral Porter was writing Secretary of the Navy Gideon Welles on Thursday, April 14. During their attack at Blair's Landing, he reported, the Confederates' "hootings and actions baffled description . . . [They] fought with such desperation and courage against certain destruction that it could only be accounted for in one way. Our opinions were verified on inspection of some of the bodies of the slain, the men actually smelling of Louisiana rum."[2]

How those bodies were inspected, given that no federals went ashore, history does not record. Otherwise, Porter gave a fair summary of events north of Grand Ecore since the troops had marched toward Mansfield and his flotilla had steamed upriver a week earlier.

But on the same day Porter wrote another report to Gideon Welles, one clearly intended for the secretary of the navy's eyes only:

> *Accompanying this is a report on my expedition up Red River* [he began]. *In that report I touched lightly on army affairs from prudential motives, not deeming it prudent to give to the public all the facts connected with the case*
> *. . .*
>
> *The army here has met with a great defeat, no matter what the generals*

try to make of it . . . The whole affair has been seriously mismanaged . . .

When I arrived here I found a bad state of affairs, the army much demoralized, and the men talking loudly of the mismanagement which thinned their numbers . . . It was well we came up, for I am convinced the rebels would have attacked this broken army at Grand Ecore had we not been here to cover them. I do not believe our army would be in a condition to meet them . . . I can get away from here . . . but if I was to leave altogether, it would be a stain upon the Navy for all time to come, and would be followed by a disastrous retreat of the army with much loss of men . . .

I do not see why a fleet should not have the protection of an army as well as an army the protection of a fleet. If we are left here aground, our communications will be cut off and we will have to destroy the vessels. I do not intend to destroy a rowboat if it can be helped, and if the proper course is pursued we will lose nothing. The army should hold this place until the last man can stand . . .

I wish the department would give me its views without delay . . . I could not leave this army now without disgracing myself forever, and when running a risk in [the Army's] cause, I do not want to be deserted . . .[3]

Porter also wrote Sherman on April 14. His main purpose was to commend A. J. Smith and his men and to explain the way matters stood:

You will no doubt feel much disappointed at not having General A. J. Smith's division returned to you in the time expected, but you will be reconciled when I tell you that the safety of this army and my whole fleet depends on his staying here. His is the only part of the army not demoralized, and if he was to leave there would be a most disastrous retreat. The army has been shamefully beaten by the rebels. There is no disguising the fact, notwithstanding the general commanding and his staff try to make a victory. Your part of it maintained its reputation and saved the army from being beaten in a two days' fight . . . You know my opinion of political generals. It is a crying sin to put the lives of thousands in the hands of such men, and the time has come when we should put a stop to it. This army is almost in a state of mutiny and not fit to go into a fight. They would follow A. J. Smith, though, anywhere.[4]

Porter included a statement in his letter to Sherman—"I am not sure that Banks will not sacrifice my vessels now to expediency; that is, his necessities"—that evidently he had made also to some of his officers. Lieutenant Commander Tom Selfridge put the question to Banks, apparently, for on April 17 the general gave him this answer in a letter:

We are here under instructions from the Government to move upon Shreveport in cooperation with the forces of General Steele. General Steele fails to cooperate with us as far as we can learn, and thus far renders us no assistance . . . With the cooperation of his forces, our occupation of Shreveport is certain and immediate. It is impossible at this time to say whether we shall receive this cooperation or not. Until it is ascertained definitely that this part of the plan of the Government at Washington will fall through, and that my force is insufficient to advance farther upon this line against the enemy, who appears to be in full force, I shall entertain no thought of a retrograde movement, certainly not if it leaves the navy in any danger. No such purpose is contemplated now.[5]

Earlier, in the message Porter received at Loggy Bayou, Banks had all but blamed his decision to withdraw from Pleasant Hill on the navy. His land column, he said, "being unable to communicate with the forces from the river, has been compelled to retreat."[6] Now Banks was holding Steele responsible for the failure so far of what the general was pleased to term "instructions from the Government"—as though he had not made any decisions of his own that had bearing on the fate of the campaign. Moreover, Selfridge may well have wondered how Banks could continue to speak of occupying Shreveport at a time when he was fortifying Grand Ecore in anticipation of a siege by an army he believed totaled twenty-five thousand rebels.

In fact, Taylor had less than five thousand. And he had sent some of them below Alexandria to harass Union steamer traffic on the lower Red River.[7]

By Sunday, April 17, Nathaniel Banks had convinced himself that "the campaign is of greater importance than was generally anticipated at its commencement, and also that immediate success, with a concentration of our forces, is within our reach"—or so he wrote General-in-Chief Ulysses Grant, with a copy to General Halleck in Washington. In that message Banks made no reference to his recent humiliations. Instead, he made a plea for reinforcement by Steele, justifying it with the claim that he was holding "[the rebels'] full strength for the defense of their position, relieving entirely Missouri and Arkansas." Another argument General Banks advanced in favor of the concentration of federal efforts was that low water in the Red River "deprives us substantially of the assistance of the gunboats, leaving us to depend entirely to depend on the strength of our land forces . . . above the point now occupied."[8]

Ten days would pass before Grant received this remarkable proposal. In

Major General Frederick Steele, USV

the meantime, news of General Banks' defeat at Sabine Crossroads and retreat from Pleasant Hill was reaching the War Department in Washington—some of it in the form of telegrams from Frederick Steele dated April
17 and 18, more of it relayed to Secretary of War Edwin M. Stanton by
Brigadier General Mason Brayman, the commander of the garrison at
Cairo, Illinois.

According to a wire Brayman sent to Washington on April 21, Brigadier
General John M. Corse had just returned from a visit to Banks at Grand
Ecore; Sherman had sent Corse there to remind Banks that A. J. Smith's
ten thousand troops were to be returned by April 15 and were to be loaded
on transports for movement east of the Mississippi without further delay.
Corse was carrying Admiral Porter's letter to Sherman (the one in which
Porter advocated leaving Smith with Banks) when he reached Cairo.
Banks, Corse reported to Stanton and General-in-Chief Grant through
Brayman, had lost four thousand men, more than two hundred wagons,
and sixteen artillery pieces.[9] General Grant, then with Major General
George G. Meade's Army of the Potomac near Culpeper, Virginia, wired
General Halleck a copy of the facts he had received from Cairo the next
day and made these comments:

> You can see from General Brayman's despatch to me something of General
> Banks' disaster. I have been satisfied for the last nine months that to keep
> General Banks in command was to neutralize a large force and to support it
> most expensively. Although I do not insist on it, I think the best interests of
> the service demand that [Major General Joseph J.] Reynolds should be
> placed in command at once, and that he name his own successor to the
> command of New Orleans.[10]

By order of Secretary of War Stanton, Halleck showed Grant's wire to
Abraham Lincoln. "The President replied," Halleck telegraphed Grant on
April 23, "that he must delay acting on it for the present."[11] Two days later
Halleck had more for the general-in-chief:

> I have just seen Admiral Porter's despatch dated Grand Ecore, April 14, to
> the Navy Department. He says, whatever may be said, the army there has
> met with a great defeat, and is much demoralized. He speaks in strong
> terms of Banks' mismanagement . . .[12]

On that same day Grant replied: "I would send orders to General Steele
to return to Little Rock; to General Banks to return himself immediately to
New Orleans," and to leave his troops under the command of the senior

officer present with orders to "see the gunboats safely out of the Red River as soon as possible."[13] In another message to Halleck that day General Grant mentioned two private letters he had just received from New Orleans "giving deplorable reports of General Banks' mismanagement." Those letters, said Grant, "clearly show all his disasters to be attributable to his incompetency."[14]

By April 28 Grant had received Banks' proposal regarding consolidation of Steele's troops with his own. Acting for Grant, Chief of Staff Halleck had already started orders on their way west of the Mississippi directing General Steele to head back to Little Rock and General Banks to turn his army over to William Franklin and go to New Orleans. On the next day Grant wired Halleck: "General Banks, by his failure, has absorbed ten thousand veteran troops that should now be with General Sherman, and thirty thousand of his own, that would have been moving toward Mobile, and this without accomplishing any good result."[15] And in another message the same day Grant added: "On due reflection I do not see that anything can be done this spring with troops west of the Mississippi, except on that side."[16]

The general-in-chief had gone as far as he could toward relieving Nathaniel Banks from field command; the Bobbin Boy's fate now depended on what the President decided.

+≡≡≡≡+

Richard Taylor was running a gigantic bluff, one so successful that Yankees working on Grand Ecore's fortifications told General Franklin, when he assured them the federal army could whip the rebels without all that protection, "We have been defeated once, and we think we will look out for ourselves."[17]

Inside the semicircle of entrenchments General Banks declared two officers scapegoats: Charles P. Stone, his chief of staff, and Albert Lee. Both were relieved of their duties and ordered to leave forthwith.

Considering the fact that General Stone had been thrown into prison for 189 days 1862, spending most of that time in solitary confinement, never having been allowed due process of law by the Radical Joint Congressional Committee on the Conduct of the War and Secretary of War Edwin Stanton, it was admirable (and also surprising) for Banks to have asked for the services of this utterly—if unfairly—disgraced officer back in April 1863. "Having entire confidence in [General Stone's] zeal and ability," wrote Banks at the time, "I will hold myself responsible to the Government for his conduct in the future."[18]

On the surface, Stone's subsequent performance as Banks' chief of staff had appeared to be satisfactory. Yet the two men had nothing more in common than origins in Massachusetts. Stone was a West Pointer, Mexican War veteran, a protege of now-retired Lieutenant General Winfield Scott.[19] Banks, who had once told his wife, "I think I might become somebody," was tragically out of place in uniform.

"General Banks and General Stone were not on good terms," William Dwight (Banks' close friend and Stone's successor as chief of staff) told the Committee on the Conduct of the War in 1865, adding: "General Stone's judgment was excessively bad." And in response to a question regarding responsibility for placing Albert Lee's two- to three-mile-long wagon train between his cavalry and the nearest infantry units on the way to Sabine Crossroads on April 8, Dwight testified:

It is the duty of the chief of staff to issue the orders of march for the troops, and to attend to all the details of the movement of troops. It does not appear, from anything that I have ever seen, that this was attended to in the way it ought to have been, or that the influence in these matters which ought to have pertained to General Stone did pertain to him.[20]

That was the answer the Congressional Radicals who had unjustly persecuted Stone in 1861 wanted to hear. However, William Franklin was nearer the truth when he told Senator Benjamin F. Wade's committee that *he* accepted responsibility for the mistake.[21] In fact, as the general commanding, Banks had the duty to oversee such undertakings.

Whether William Dwight's influence caused Charles Stone's removal would never be as clear as his motive was suspicious. And another question remained open: Had Banks sought to deflect blame from himself for Sabine Crossroads and its consequences by banishing a man who had no defenders in Washington?

Curiously, since well before General Banks relieved Stone, orders from the War Department had been on the way to him. On April 4, Secretary of War Edwin Stanton revoked his commission as a brigadier general of volunteers and directed him to report to Cairo, Illinois, to await reassignment. Stanton gave no reason for this action, which was consistent with his earlier contemptible refusal to recognize Stone's rights under military law and the Constitution.[22]

General Banks told the Committee on the Conduct of the War that he relieved Brigadier General Lee not on account of Sabine Crossroads but "because the general officers expressed to me so positively their want of confidence in the organization and condition of the cavalry, and advised so earnestly a change."[23] In view of Nathaniel Banks' history at several critical points during the campaign of being receptive to advice earnestly given, this explanation seemed plausible.

However, William Dwight, one of the general officers to whom Banks was known to listen, tied Lee and defeat at Sabine Crossroads together in his testimony: "I consider our force of cavalry, mounted infantry, &c., was badly commanded," he said, "that the officer commanding it did not understand the manner of leading an advance, of obtaining proper information concerning the enemy." Lee's force, Dwight continued, "stood dormant in the presence of the enemy until the enemy completely enveloped it." And he added: "Whoever directed that on our part was completely incapable."[24]

Earlier, Lee had told the committee that he held his position while awaiting infantry reinforcements, which he had been requesting since before he made contact with the rebels. That Dwight's allegation might lack credibility was reflected in the next question his interrogator, Congressman Daniel Gooch of Massachusetts, put to him: "From whom do you derive the information which enables you to state that our forces stood dormant until the enemy enveloped them?" From the official reports, Dwight responded.[25]

By early 1865 when General Banks appeared before Bluff Ben Wade's committee, his attitude toward the cavalry's commander had mellowed. He regretted relieving Lee, he said. "He was active, willing, and brave, and suffered, more or less unjustly, as all of us did, for being connected with that affair."[26]

⊹━◆━⊹

At Grand Ecore, secure behind the fortifications his troops had prepared and with Porter's gunboats there on the river to provide covering fire if and when needed, General Banks no longer had to worry about being totally destroyed by Taylor's supposed twenty-five thousand. But unless Banks obtained and kept control of most of the state, news of his whipping at Sabine Crossroads and of his withdrawal from Pleasant Hill to Grand Ecore would hardly please his superiors in faraway Washington; indeed, in these circumstances, how could the president be encouraged regarding Louisiana's prospects of being the model for the early restoration of Union-occupied Southern states?

"We have more to fear from our friends," Banks had said nearly two years earlier, "than from the bayonets of our enemies." Although the context was different now, that statement was more valid than ever.

General Banks had not reached Shreveport by April 10 and he had been unable to return A. J. Smith's ten thousand men to Sherman by April 15. Could he get to Shreveport by April 30, Grant's deadline? If not, his orders were to abandon the campaign. And could Banks do even that, if either insufficient water flowing over the mile-long rapids at Alexandria or Taylor's forces trapped Porter's gunboats?

And there were also those friends of Banks in New England, the powerful political supporters who were depending on him to capture the cotton they needed to keep even a small fraction of their textile mills in operation. So far, Porter and his prize money-crazed sailors had stolen most of the bales; Confederate plantation owners had burned the rest. No cotton, no hope for the Bobbin Boy's presidential ambitions.

Yet a little time remained; Banks was reluctant to declare that capturing Shreveport was impossible, although hardly any of his generals had any desire to face Richard Taylor again and Admiral Porter's mind seemed to be only on trying to raise the ironclad *Eastport*, which had hit a Confederate torpedo (submerged mine) four miles below Grand Ecore nearly a week earlier. Everything depended, apparently, on whether Frederick Steele would come down from wherever in Arkansas he was and reinforce him. However, General Halleck had failed to appoint anyone overall commander of the operation. All Banks could do was *ask* Steele to join him, actually to save the campaign, and this much he had done. Truly, now Banks had more to fear from Washington and Arkansas and New England, and possibly even from his own officers and men right there in Grand Ecore, than from Dick Taylor and his army.

Porter had made Steele's cooperation vital by insisting that he could not support another attempt to reach Shreveport as long as the water in the river remained as low as it had been on the way to Grand Ecore from Loggy Bayou. Well, the water level had continued to fall; indeed, now the admiral would be lucky to get his whole flotilla as far southward as Alexandria. The possibility that conditions in the river would get even worse suggested that Banks could not remain at Grand Ecore very much longer. He had to place considerable weight also on General-in-Chief Grant's combination of an order and a warning, which he had received as far back as March 26:

> If you do not accomplish the object of your expedition, by the occupation of Shreveport, within ten days from the time fixed by General Sherman [for the return of A. J. Smith's divisions], you will return to New Orleans, even if you have to abandon entirely the expedition upon which you have entered; and if it takes you beyond the 1st of May to return to New Orleans, I shall regret that you ever started upon the expedition at all.[27]

N

PORTER

Grand Ecore

Natchitoches

WHARTON

TAYLOR

Cane River

Red River

BANKS

Cloutierville

POLIGNAC

Monett's Ferry

BEE

Banks' Escape From Grand Ecore

Later, General Banks would testify before Ben Wade's Committee on the Conduct of the War: "It became absolutely certain that if we did get [to Shreveport], we could not get down again; and it was certain that if the army and the fleet were destroyed, we endangered if we did not lose, the navigation of the Mississippi and the possession of New Orleans. I therefore determined that, as soon as we could get the fleet clear, I would return to New Orleans under the order of General Grant."[28]

Encouraged by Porter's optimism regarding the *Eastport* now that two pump boats were working at the scene, General Banks began planning his withdrawal to Alexandria. He was still laboring under the impression that Dick Taylor outnumbered him, so he decided to use A. J. Smith's divisions as his rear guard and to have Franklin's units lead the way southward.[29]

The Red River made its way toward Alexandria in a roughly south-southwesterly series of loops. Just below Grand Ecore the Cane River branched off west of the Red and for thirty miles or so flowed parallel to it at a distance from it of not more than six miles. After passing Cloutierville and Monett's Ferry, the Cane rejoined the Red at a town called Colfax. Banks' army would be taking a road running down the island formed by the Cane and the Red, leaving it at Monett's Ferry and then proceeding directly to Alexandria. On the island stretches the road was near the Cane and beyond the range of the guns on Porter's tinclads on the Red; even so, the admiral assigned several of them the task of keeping pace with the army's advance.[30]

A. J. Smith occupied nearby Natchitoches on April 20 to distract Taylor's attention while the rest of Banks' army prepared to retreat. The march southward began late the next day. As a farewell gesture the federal troops burned what there was of Grand Ecore and the supplies they had been unable to take with them.[31]

General Taylor, too, had been doing some planning although his department commander had left him with pitifully few units. His best chance to maul Banks again, it seemed, would come when the Yankees reached Cloutierville, about twenty miles down the Cane River from Natchitoches. Taylor ordered Polignac to place his greatly depleted division on the Cane's western bank across from the town. John Wharton, who had replaced the much-missed Tom Green, would go into position east of Cloutierville roughly half way between the Red and the Cane; this would put Wharton in rear of the federals as they passed on their way to Monett's Ferry. At Monett's Hamilton Bee and his cavalry would be waiting on the bluffs to block Banks' escape. And if Banks should try to use the Red River instead as his getaway route, Liddell's force would be on the east bank near the junction of the Red and the Cane.[32]

But could fewer than five thousand men in four separated elements, no matter how skillfully deployed, stop four or five times that many?

+—◇—+

Earlier, many of the men in A. J. Smith's divisions had seen war waged in ways different from those experienced by other soldiers, for they had participated in the sweep General Sherman's army made in February from Vicksburg to Meridian. Afterward Sherman had boasted that his troops had "made a swath of desolation fifty miles broad across the State of Mississippi which the present generation will not forget."[33]

Cump had decided that the quickest way to end the fighting was to destroy the basic resources on which the Confederacy depended for its continuation, to make ordinary Southerners feel the consequences of rebellion so directly and so acutely that they would cease supporting it forthwith. "When the provisions, forage, horses, mules, wagons, &c. are used by our enemy," he wrote, "it is clearly our duty and right to take them, because otherwise they might be used against us."[34] Depriving rebels of property was likely to end the war sooner, he believed, than killing them.

From their first day ashore in Louisiana a month ago A. J. Smith's men had looted and burned the farms and homes of civilians at every opportunity. Some of those soldiers might have committed such acts in any event; wars have a way of loosening inhibitions; and in any large body of men there are likely to be certain percentages of criminals. But Cump had elevated the kind of cruelty unleashed in Mississippi to the level of legitimacy possessed by military operations against armed forces. And as Nathaniel Banks' army retreated southward along the Cane River bound for Alexandria, Smith's federals added torching and robbing every rebel house and farm in their path to their duties as rear guards.

Leading the very long column and screening its flanks as it retreated were three brigades of cavalry. Because of the movement's late starting time on Thursday, April 21, and Banks' uneasiness regarding reports that Dick Taylor was not far away, the march continued well into the night. Cavalrymen, then, and not A. J. Smith's arsonists, had the honor of burning the first of the thousands of houses along the way that would be left in smoldering ruin. Those fires, of course, literally blazed the trail for the rest of the army to follow.[35]

Behind the troopers came an infantry division commanded by Brigadier

General Henry W. Birge, a force that included the thirty-six hundred men General Banks—during the confusion following Sabine Crossroads and Pleasant Hill—had ordered Brigadier General Cuvier Grover to bring up to Grand Ecore from Alexandria, where they had been providing security.[36] Also with Birge was a brigade that had been mauled at Pleasant Hill, now led by Colonel Francis Fessenden. Trains were next, with Franklin's infantry just ahead of A. J. Smith's rear guard.[37]

Placing his best troops in the column's rear proved to have been a prudent move on Nathaniel Banks' part, for the mounted infantry General Taylor led in pursuit were appalled and enraged by the evidence of depravity the Yankees had left in their wake. Taylor had been in Shreveport writing reports and obtaining supplies for the pitifully few men Kirby Smith had allowed him to retain, but he reached Grand Ecore at about the time Banks' retreat was beginning. Knowing that the only road the federals could take required them to cross the Cane at Monett's Ferry, forty miles from Grand Ecore, Taylor sent word to General Bee to prepare diligently for the enemy's arrival.[38]

Major General John Wharton, commander of Taylor's pursuit force, was a Texan who had won distinction as a leader of cavalry at Shiloh and Stones River.[39] Now he had the unenviable challenge of replacing the widely admired Tom Green. His mission was to press Banks' rear guard and to punish its miscreants.[40]

There was a chance that Banks might try to cross the Cane River at Cloutierville and use a road running westward from there as an escape route instead moving on southward to Monett's Ferry. Brigadier General Camille Armand Jules Marie Prince de Polignac's division was waiting near Cloutierville to prevent this.[41] But Taylor had just received reinforcements from Texas—seven hundred mounted infantrymen under Brigadier General William Steele, a West Point graduate who had served in the "Old Army" for twenty-one years (a period that included the Seminole and Mexican wars) but whose assignments so far as a Confederate officer had been in New Mexico and the Indian Territory—and he sent this force to bolster Polignac's.[42]

Then occurred a series of incidents that generated the deep hostility toward Northerners that Louisianans and Texans would feel during the Reconstruction years and for generations to come. That the devastation the retreating federals caused on the island formed by the Cane and Red Rivers was intentional and premeditated was indicated by a passage in one of T. Kilby Smith's letters:

The inhabitants here about are pretty tolerably frightened; our Western troops are tired of shilly shally, and this year they will deal their blows very heavily. Past kindnesses and forbearance [have] not been appreciated or understood; frequently ridiculed. The people now will be terribly scourged.[43]

One of Kilby Smith's soldiers recalled that he and men with him burned every building along their route on April 22. Dead hogs, cows, horses, and other farm animals lined the road after the Yankees passed.[44] "At night," wrote another veteran of the retreat, "the burning buildings mark our pathway. As far as the eye can reach, we see in front new fires breaking out, and in the rear the dying embers tell the tale of war." But this federal author placed the blame where he believed it belonged: "The wanton and useless destruction of property has earned [A. J. Smith's] command a lasting disgrace," he said, and he added that "In order that the stigma of rendering houseless and homeless innocent women and children may not rest upon us, be it recorded that not only the Commander of the army, but Division and Brigade commanders have issued orders reprobating it, and threatening offenders with instant death."[45] After the war Richard Taylor made this comment:

From the universal testimony of citizens, I learned that General Banks and the officers and men of the 19th Corps, Eastern troops, exerted themselves to prevent these outrages, and that the perpetrators were the men of General A. J. Smith of Sherman's army.[46]

John Wharton's Texans were the only forces positioned to attack the marauders but they were outnumbered and the Yankee retreat was rapid: Banks marched his army from Grand Ecore to Cloutierville, thirty-two miles, without stopping.[47] Clearly, the only vengeance Taylor's men could wreak would be exacted, if any were to be exacted at all, down at Monett's Ferry.

"I had a faint idea," David Dixon Porter said in a report to Secretary of the Navy Gideon Welles dated April 28, "that our army were about to fall back on Alexandria, when it would become necessary to destroy the *Eastport* or, perhaps lose some other vessels."[48] Raising the gunboat, the largest and most powerful in his flotilla, had been a high priority with the admiral since the warship had been submerged to its gun deck by a collision with a Confederate torpedo about four miles down the Red River from Grand Ecore. But by removing the *Eastport's* guns, and with the aid of two pump boats Porter had ordered up from Alexandria and several days of hard work by Lieutenant Commander S. Ledyard Phelps and his crew, the *Eastport* was floated again on Thursday, April 21.[49] During that day and the next, the transport *Champion No. 3* towed her toward Alexandria for twenty miles; then, to the dismay of Porter and Phelps, the *Eastport* ran aground on Friday evening and again on Saturday, April 23.

"I determined that I would never leave this vessel to her fate," Porter wrote Secretary Welles, "as long as the commander felt a hope of getting her down."[50] Phelps had particularly strong affection for the *Eastport*. After the capture of Fort Henry in February 1862, he had led a flotilla consisting of the *Lexington* and two other gunboats up the Tennessee River; at a place called Cerro Gordo he took possession of the vessel, earlier among the fastest steamboats on the Mississippi, then about halfway through the process of being converted into a Confederate ironclad. Phelps' *Eastport* had been the pride of Porter's Mississippi Squadron ever since. But she had proved too large and too heavy to make it over Alexandria's rapids without blocking access to the upper Red River for several days back in March, and she was too bulky to be used in the cruise up to Loggy Bayou, and lately it had been difficult for her captain to keep count of the number of times she had gotten caught on snags or sandbars, rocks, and submerged logs.[51]

The *Eastport* ran "hard aground" again on Tuesday, April 26. She had gone only a few miles in nearly a week, and this discouraged even Phelps. The shortage of time precluded efforts to lighten the *Eastport* by removing her iron plates. Scouts sent downstream returned and reported that the river ahead was too shallow for a boat with such a deep draft. With great reluctance, Porter gave the order to destroy the vessel.[52]

Commander Phelps sent the crew over to the *Fort Hindman*, the gunboat that had made one final effort to pull the *Eastport* free and had failed. "I took off everything movable and of value," he wrote later in his report, "and then placed a prepared can and 8 barrels of gunpowder under the foot of her forward casemate, which an operator tried to explode by electricity. Failing in his attempts, a similar amount of powder was placed in her stern and other barrels of powder were put about her machinery, so as effectually to destroy her, and trains were laid fore and aft the vessel . . . "[53]

Just previous to blowing up the *Eastport*, Porter's account continued, "the rebels selected this moment to make their attack, and, rising suddenly from the bank, opened on our little squadron with twelve hundred muskets and then made a rush to board the *Cricket*. The enemy, however, were properly met and repelled."[54]

After that, aboard the *Eastport* Commander Phelps—who would be the last man to leave her—applied the match to the trains leading to three thousand pounds of powder, fifty kegs of it. "Seven different explosions followed," Admiral Porter reported, "and then flames burst forth in every direction. The vessel was completely destroyed, as perfect a wreck as ever was made by gunpowder."[55]

Steaming downriver in the midday hours after the last pieces of the *Eastport's* iron, wood, and other debris fell to earth, David Dixon Porter must have found, was nigh-pleasant. He sat on the *Cricket's* upper deck, dividing his attention between a book and the four boats following the *Cricket: Champion No. 3*, then *Champion No. 5* lashed to the tinclad *Juliet*, and finally the *Fort Hindman*, hindmost in the flotilla.[56]

Porter may well have recalled the boasting done by a Confederate corporal captured during the rebels' attempt to board the *Cricket*, hours before, while he and Ledyard Phelps had been trying to save the *Eastport*. Up ahead on a bluff, the prisoner had assured the admiral, was a force of at least two thousand men with eighteen guns. The grayback soldier was bluffing, or so Porter decided; and sure enough, no Confederates had been seen on the west bank since the flotilla had left the remains of the *Eastport*.[57]

Even so, Porter had taken the precaution of placing gun batteries forward and near the stern. But early vigilance had given way to drowsiness, and both crews like the admiral had succumbed to the pleasures of a quiet boatride on a perfect spring afternoon.

Well, Porter had not quite succumbed. On the high ground west of the river he thought he saw the glint of sunlight on metal. "Corridge!" he yelled to the *Cricket's* captain, "give those fellows in the bushes a two-second shell!"[58]

Those fellows in the bushes were indeed Confederates, although not necessarily the ones the corporal had warned the admiral about. This force from Polignac's division had two hundred infantrymen, not two thousand, and only four guns: two twelve-pounders, smoothbore, and two howitzers. At Blair's Landing, where Tom Green had been killed while attacking a Yankee flotilla, it had not been possible to depress the artillery pieces' tubes enough to blast the invaders' ships out of the damp sand. Here, near Colfax where the Cane River rejoined the Red, Captain Florian Cornay's gunners could hit anything that floated. Their instructions were to let the first boat get right under them, and then to open fire; the rest of the vessels would pile up behind it. And as the artillery filled the air with solid shot, shrapnel, canister, and grape, the infantrymen along the bluff would shower the federal boats' decks with a hailstorm of minié balls too thick for any sailor who left cover to live through.[59]

Admiral Porter was ordering the battery on *Cricket's* bow to fire another round when the little tinclad shuddered from the impact of the rebel artillery's direct hits plunging into her. Prudently, he ran for shelter. *Cricket*, he assumed, would soon be downriver enough to be beyond the range of the rebel battery. But suddenly the tinclad's engines stopped. Her captain had given that order so that his ship's guns could engage the enemy's.[60] What happened next was described by Porter in a report to Navy Secretary Welles:

> I corrected this mistake and got headway on the vessel again, but not soon enough to avoid the pelting shower of shot and shell which the enemy poured into us—every shot going through and through us, clearing all our decks in a moment. Finding the guns not firing rapidly, I stepped on the gun deck to see what was the matter. As I stepped down, the after gun was struck with a shell and disabled, and every man at the gun killed and wounded. At the same moment the crew from the forward gun was swept away by a shell exploding, and the men were wounded in the fire room, leaving only one man to fire up. I made up a gun's crew from the contrabands [freed slaves], who fought the gun to the last moment. Finding that the engine did not move, I went into the engine room, and found the chief engineer killed, whose place was soon supplied by an assistant. I then went to the pilot house and found that a shot had gone through it and wounded one of the pilots. I took charge of the vessel, and as the battery was a very heavy one I determined to pass it, which was done under the heaviest fire I ever witnessed. I attempted to turn her head upstream to attack with our two bow guns, the only guns left, but as this was impracticable, I let her drift down around the point and shelled the enemy's batteries from the rear.[61]

Porter took the *Cricket* downstream intending to find his ironclads and send them up to help the *Juliet*, lashed to the *Champion No. 5*; the *Champion No. 3*; and the *Fort Hindman*, still above the Confederate battery. "Unfortunately," the admiral confessed to Welles, "I ran on shore a short time after passing the batteries."[62]

Back under the fire of the Confederates' guns, Lieutenant Commander Phelps was in charge of the *Juliet* and *Champion No. 5* though his men from the *Eastport* were on the *Fort Hindman*. He was obliged to watch, horrified, from a distance as a rebel round blew up the transport downstream from him, the *Champion No. 3*.[63] Confederate Colonel Joseph L. Brent reported certain potentially embarrassing details neither Phelps nor Admiral Porter included in their accounts:

> The transport Champion No. 3 *was struck in the boiler by a solid shot and*

was enveloped in hot steam and water. This transport was loaded with near 200 Negroes, consisting of men, women, and children taken from the plantations above, and most recklessly and cruelly attempted, under the convoy of gunboats and under actual fire, to be run through the lines of our army.[64]

That single twelve-pound shot, Colonel Brent declared, "was probably the most fatal shot fired during the war, producing the death of 187 human beings, over one-half instantaneously, and the remainder within twenty-four hours. All on board except three perished by the most frightful of deaths, and the steamer fell into our hands."[65]

With the *Cricket* around the bend and the *Champion No. 3* out of action, Confederate Captain Cornay turned his four guns on the *Juliet* and the *Champion No. 5*, severing the tinclad's steam pipe and tiller ropes. In the confusion crewmen on the *Champion No. 5* began cutting the lines holding the vessels together; with only one remaining, pilot William Maitland jumped from the *Juliet* to the transport's deck, ran to its abandoned pilothouse, and steamed upriver with the disabled gunboat in tow. The *Fort Hindman* provided covering fire until the three vessels were far enough beyond the range of the rebel guns to stop for repairs, a task that would require much of the night.[66]

The next morning, Wednesday, April 27, Commander Phelps ordered the two gunboats and the transport to run the rebel batteries that had all but destroyed Porter's flotilla the day before. Shortly after getting under way the *Juliet* hit a snag and had to turn back upriver for repairs. Those proved in vain, for when the tinclad came within range the Confederate gunners blew away much of her superstructure and damaged her machinery. The *Fort Hindman* also drew heavy fire; a round hit her pilothouse and destroyed it, carrying away her tiller ropes and rendering the vessel unmanageable—as was the *Juliet*.[67]

During the night the Confederates had placed the battered hulk that had been the *Champion No. 3* in the middle of the river to block the three remaining Yankee boats. On Wednesday morning both the *Fort Hindman* and the *Juliet* managed to sweep around the obstacle, but the transport *Champion No. 5* nosed into the eastern bank and was captured. In Confederate Colonel Joseph Brent's words: "After a short engagement the gunboats, receiving serious damage from [Cornay's] heroic battery, ingloriously fled and left the transport exposed to so fatal a fire that she soon sunk and became our prize."[68]

Unlike General Banks, whose reports often reflected only those bits of information that put his performance in favorable light, Admiral Porter was candid (if a little boastful) in what he wrote Gideon Welles:

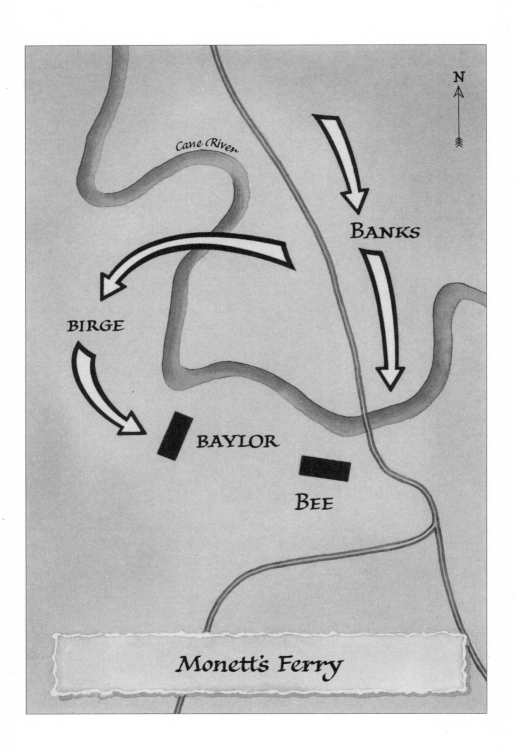

N

Cane River

BANKS

BIRGE

BAYLOR

BEE

Monett's Ferry

No vessels were ever better fought, and none of this class (mere thread pa-
per vessels) were ever under so hot a fire. In five minutes the Cricket *was*
struck 38 times with solid shot and shell, with a loss of 25 killed and
wounded, half her crew. The Juliet *about the same, with 15 killed and*
wounded. The Fort Hindman *lost 3 killed and 4 or 5 wounded.*[69]

Nor did Porter seek to evade responsibility: "I may have lacked judgment in not blowing up the *Eastport* sooner, when I found that we were a
secondary consideration to the army," he admitted, "but as I had stayed behind to see the last transport through safely, I could not do less with one of
my own vessels."[70]

Porter was unable to keep in communication with the army, he conceded, "as they marched along faster than I calculated (40 miles in one day,
when I supposed they would only go 20), [and] I was more in their rear
than I should have been. This arose from my desire to save the *Eastport*,
and hoping that some signal success on the part of the army (which I felt
confident was able to whip all the rebels in this part of the country) would
dispose of the enemy altogether."[71]

In the two days of wrecking Porter's flotilla Confederate losses were one
sharpshooter wounded and one officer killed, Captain Cornay.

<hr>

Writing Secretary Welles from Alexandria on April 28, Admiral Porter
said he was very much surprised that he had any gunboats left, "considering
all the difficulties encountered."[72] Indeed his worst fears might have mate-
rialized if he had not devoted so much time to saving the *Eastport*, for Major General Nathaniel Banks' army had drawn the bulk of Richard Taylor's
forces well below the scenes of naval disaster several days before those
events occurred.

Actually, Banks had little choice of speeds for his "skeedaddle," for
Taylor's cavalrymen—intent on revenge for the Yankee arsonists' depreda-
tions—were pressing A. J. Smith's rear guard vigorously. Word spread
throughout the federal ranks that Smith's men might not be able to withstand the rebels' assaults. This had the ironic effect of complicating life for
the Confederate commander, however, for he wanted to make certain per-
sonally that Hamilton Bee had made wise use of the terrain and his resources at Monett's Ferry and time did not allow Taylor to ride down
there.[73]

At Monett's Ferry the Cane River made an abrupt turn from a southeasterly course to a northeasterly one before joining the Red River near Colfax. Bluffs and rolling hills south of the Cane were nigh-ideal for blocking or at least delaying any force attempting to use the ferry on its way toward Alexandria. Creeks flowing into the Cane from its south side gave defenders additional opportunities to slaughter Yankees.

Hamilton Bee deployed his cavalry and artillery as best he could on the high ground overlooking the ferry and the road the federals would most likely be taking toward Alexandria. But he had only about a thousand men and he might be facing as many as twenty thousand; such was the result of General Kirby Smith's having taken Taylor's infantry divisions to Arkansas. Even so, Bee was well aware of the importance of his serving as the anvil on which Wharton's cavalry and Polignac's remnants could hammer the retreating Union army to pieces.[74]

Mindful of the pressure Wharton's troopers were applying to A. J. Smith's rear guard, and acting with more prudence than he had often been wont to do, Nathaniel Banks ordered Brigadier General William Emory to move the rest of the federal forces past Monett's Ferry. Well before dawn on Saturday, April 23, Emory sent cavalry led by Brigadier General Richard Arnold southward, backed by infantry. By sunrise blueclad troopers, under Albert Lee's command earlier, had pushed Confederate skirmishers south of the Cane.

Emory considered Bee's line too formidable to break with frontal assault. Colonel E. J. Davis with a brigade of cavalry rode eastward along the Cane in search of another crossing site but no suitable one was found. Stopped by the river on the left but encouraged by a black man's assurance that there was a ford about two miles upstream from the ferry, Emory then tried the right. Henry Birge's brigades found the Cane's waters waist-deep but they made the crossing without much difficulty and moved southward and eastward through rough country in search of Bee's western flank.[75]

In anticipation of such a possibility General Bee had sent Colonel George W. Baylor and more men than he could spare over to cover the wooded hills and ravines up the Cane River from Monett's Ferry. After falling back several times Baylor drew the federals into an ambush in which Confederate artillery and rifle fire stunned Birge's attackers and thinned their ranks. Baylor's repulse all but demoralized the maneuvering force. Men running to the rear in panic were further unnerved when fleeing cavalrymen rode through them. One officer, attempting to get his men up and moving forward through the withering Confederate fire, yelled, "Stand up! For God's sake, stand up like men!" But to hold the Yankees, George Baylor needed reinforcements and artillery fire that only General Bee could provide.

Hamilton Bee, meanwhile, had been given a report (which proved false) that Union troops had crossed the Cane River downstream. Believing there were Yankees on both his flanks and watching blueclad forces on the river's north bank massing as though they were preparing to attack his own line, the Confederate commander apparently took counsel of his fears. Instead of strengthening Baylor, who seemed to have turned back the only serious federal threat, Bee ordered him to disengage and withdraw. Bee then compounded his blunder by retreating to the west on a road that led to a place called Beasley's—and by so doing, leaving the road from Monett's Ferry southward to Alexandria wide open for Nathaniel Banks' army to use.[76]

But for a time Richard Taylor's assaults on the Yankees' rear guard, together with the sound of gunfire coming from the south, had succeeded in making federals in the center of Banks' long column believe they were surrounded. His scourging of A. J. Smith's marauders, augmented by artillery, continued on Sunday, April 24, until mid-afternoon when the last of Banks' troops crossed a pontoon bridge that Union engineers and thrown across the Cane.[77]

Taylor was infuriated both by Hamilton Bee's failure to hold the high ground at Monett's Ferry and by his egregious error in not creating blocking positions on the Alexandria road to delay Banks' advance until Polignac's men and Wharton's cavalry could strike Banks' troops and wagon trains. As matters stood, the best Taylor could do was recall some of Bee's mounted infantry and combine it with cavalrymen newly arrived from Texas in pursuit of the federals all the way down the road to Alexandria.[78]

"General Bee had exhibited much personal gallantry in the charge at Pleasant Hill," Taylor wrote afterward, "but he was without experience in war, and [he] had neglected to study the ground or strengthen his position at Monett's."[79] Most of the blame for Banks' escape, of course, could be assigned to Kirby Smith's having left Taylor outnumbered five to one. But while his decision to split his pitifully small force three ways in the effort to trap Banks north of the Cane reflected Jacksonian audacity, Dick Taylor had tried to accomplish far too much with far too few men.

CHAPTER 6

THE PERNICIOUS INFLUENCE OF HUNGER

Report of Rear-Admiral Porter, U.S. Navy, to Secretary of the Navy Gideon Welles, concerning the conduct of the campaign by Major-General Banks, U.S. Army, and showing the precarious condition of the navy in the river.

Confidential.] MISSISSIPPI SQUADRON, FLAGSHIP CRICKET.
   Alexandria, La., April 28, 1864.

SIR: *I have written you an account of the operations of the fleet in these waters, but take the liberty of writing to you confidentially [regarding] the true state of affairs . . . I find myself blockaded by a fall of 3 feet of water, 3 feet 4 inches being the amount now on the falls; 7 feet being required to get over; no amount of lightening will accomplish the object.*

I have already written to you how the whole state of things has been changed by a too blind carelessness on the part of our military leaders and our retreat back to Alexandria from place to place has so demoralized General Banks' army that the troops have no confidence in anybody or anything. I do not include, however, the troops of that veteran soldier General A. J. Smith . . . Our army is now all here, with the best general (Franklin) wounded and unfit for duty in the field. General Banks seems to hold no communication with anyone, and it is impossible for me to say what he will do. I have no confidence in his promises, as he asserted in a letter, herein enclosed, that he had no intention of leaving Grand Ecore, when he had actually already made his preparations to leave . . .

The river is crowded with transports, and every gunboat I have is required to convoy them . . . The enemy are splitting up into groups of 2,000 and bringing in the artillery (with which we have supplied them) to blockade points below here, and what will be the upshot of it all I can not foretell. I know that it will be disastrous in the extreme, for this is a country in which a retreating army is completely at the mercy of an enemy . . .

Unless instructed by the Government, I do not think that General

Banks will make the least effort to save the navy blockaded here. The following vessels are above the falls and command the right of the town: Mound City, Louisville, Pittsburg, Carondelet, Chillicothe, Osage, Neosho, Ozark, Lexington, and Fort Hindman.

Those here in command of the army are entirely indifferent to the whole matter, excepting General A. J. Smith, who is sorely depressed at the prospect before us. At this moment the enemy have attacked our outposts and have driven-in our indifferent cavalry . . . Our whole army is cooped up in this town while a much inferior force is going rampant about the country making preparations to assail our helpless transports, which if caught, filled with men, would be perfect slaughterhouses.

An intelligent general could get us out of the difficulties, but I see no prospect of it now. If left here by the army, I will be obliged to destroy this fleet to prevent it falling into the enemy's hands, and you can judge of my feelings at having to perform so painful a duty. I can not conceive that the nation will permit such a sacrifice to be made . . .

Our prestige will receive a shock from which it will be long in recovering, and if the calamities I dread should overtake us the annals of the war will not present so dire a one as will have befallen us.[1]

But as Admiral Porter was contemplating the demise of his Mississippi River Squadron, General Banks could see the end of his command of the federal Department of the Gulf approaching. On April 28, the day after Banks reached Alexandria, Major General David Hunter arrived from Washington; he had been sent by General-in-Chief Grant to deliver letters prepared on April 17 directing Banks to be certain he was ready by May 1 to open the campaign to take Mobile. Since Hunter's departure General Halleck had issued orders for Banks to turn his army over to the highest- ranking officer present and to go to New Orleans, but that message had not yet reached Louisiana.[2]

Hunter realized right away that the instructions Grant had sent could not be carried out. On April 28 he started a status report of sorts on its way to the general-in-chief:

I regret very much to find affairs here in a very complicated, perplexing, and precarious situation . . . We have some six, eight, or ten gun-boats, among them two monitors, above the rapids, with no possibility of getting them out. The whole question is, then, reduced to this: Shall we destroy the gun-boats or lose the services at this critical period of the war of the 20,000 men necessary to take care of them? My opinion is, of course, to destroy the boats. Why this expedition was ordered I cannot imagine. General

Banks assures me it was undertaken against his opinion and earnest pro-
test. The result is certainly a very sad one. I shall communicate from day to
day anything of interest which may occur.[3]

Also on April 28 General Banks had provided his appraisal of the situation in a message to Admiral David Farragut, Porter's superior, in New Orleans:

There are but few boats between Alexandria and the mouth of the [Red]
river. It is desirable that you send such boats as can navigate the river for
the purpose of keeping open our communications. The enemy threatens this
line in considerable force. I beg your immediate attention to this subject.
Our situation is in no wise embarrassing, except that the fleet is detained
above the rapids, and the movements of the army are dependent on its re-
lief. The army is in excellent spirits and condition and fears nothing. The
enemy is reported in force about us, and it is quite probable that we may
have a general engagement within a few days, for which we are fully pre-
pared.[4]

　　　　　　　　　　　　　　+≡≡≡+

In mid-April, while Nathaniel Banks was at Grand Ecore talking about
making another attempt to reach Shreveport but waiting to see what (if
anything) came of his appeals for reinforcements, heavy rains were falling
everywhere but in areas that were drained by tributaries of the Red River.
Creeks in Arkansas overflowing their banks had slowed John Thayer's division as it came down from Fort Smith to join Frederick Steele's force. And
during those delays men ate rations that the commanders of those federal
columns had not expected them to consume until later in the campaign.[5]

Food shortages, rather than concern over Confederate Major General
Sterling Price's massing of his cavalry brigades, caused Steele to make a
feint toward Washington on April 12 and then turn his troops eastward on
the road to Camden.[6] Once there, Steele could fortify the town, wait for
supply trains from Little Rock and Pine Bluff to reach him with desperately
needed rations, and use Camden as a base for continuing the advance to
Louisiana and ultimately East Texas.

Hardly anything had happened as General Steele had been expecting,
suggesting that he had not been as familiar with conditions in southwestern Arkansas as Grant had assumed when he ordered him to move his
forces from Little Rock to Shreveport. His most distressing disappointment
may well have been his inability to find food and fodder along the way, for

the region was not thickly settled and guerrillas as well as rebel cavalry had kept foraging parties from operating more than a few miles from the main body.

Much earlier, though, Steele had been plagued by doubts regarding the strategy dictated from Washington, D.C. Even if he succeeded in meeting Banks in Shreveport, by going on into East Texas he would be leaving the whole state of Arkansas open to repossession by Confederates from the Indian Territory in the west and Missouri to the north. Such a calamity would make a waste of time and effort of the work Steele had done to get Arkansas ready for readmission to the Union, a task President Lincoln had given him, one he had pursued although doing so had caused him to delay his departure from Little Rock.

And then there had been the high water, most recently along the road to Camden. Teams wallowed in mud as they tried to pull wagons hub-deep in the glop. Runoff from fresh rains washed away the corduroying his men had done through stretches of swamp. And on April 14 his weary troops had to fight their way through John Marmaduke's cavalry division to reach their goal; the rear guard did not enter Camden until April 16.[7]

Some food was available in and around the town, and the federals captured a Confederate steamer on the Ouachita River that was carrying several thousand bushels of corn. But Fred Steele had more than 10,000 soldiers and close to 9,000 horses and mules to feed, and on April 17 he sent a force of 700 men with two guns along as escorts for a train of 198 wagons in order to gather provisions west of Camden. The next day he ordered roughly 400 more troops to join the foraging party, which had established a camp about eighteen miles from town. Colonel James M. Williams, whose 1st Kansas (Colored) Regiment was part of the detachment, was in command.[8]

On the morning of April 18 the train, its wagons filled with corn, bacon, women's and children's clothing and other items stolen from Arkansans' homes, geese, and hogs, had gone about four miles toward Camden when it was attacked by about three thousand Confederates led by John Marmaduke. Williams put his one thousand defenders in line of battle; he placed his 1st Kansas in the center, cavalry on each flank, and several companies in the rear of the train.

Marmaduke's forces, which included Choctaw Indians, struck Williams' line head-on and from the flank after shredding it with crossfire from his artillery. The federal troops, badly outnumbered and stunned by the ferocity of the rebels' charge, ran for their lives.[9] Later, the commander of the Choctaws described the pursuit:

I feared that the train and its contents would prove a temptation too strong for these hungry, half-clothed Choctaws, but had no trouble pressing them forward, for there was that in front and to the left more inviting to them than food or clothing—the blood of their despised enemy. They had met and routed the forces of General Thayer, the ravagers of their country, the despoilers of their homes, and the murderers of their women and children.[10]

Indeed, in this engagement near a place called Poison Spring the 1st Kansas (Colored) lost 182 of its 438 men; and of the 182 casualties, 117 were killed in action. Williams' total loss was about 300 men. He also left behind all 198 wagons and four artillery pieces. Marmaduke reported 115 men as killed, wounded, or missing. But the defeat of the federals at Poison Spring would be felt also by Steele's troops in Camden, where the now-acute food shortage was alleviated only briefly by the arrival of a wagon train from Pine Bluff.[11]

As if the news of the disaster at Poison Spring had not been discouraging enough to General Steele, on the same day (April 18) a messenger arrived from Louisiana with a verbal account of Banks' whipping at Sabine Crossroads on April 8 and subsequent retreat to Grand Ecore. The next day a courier brought Steele several letters from Banks, one of which confirmed the messenger's report. In another, Banks urged Steele to bring his army down to northern Louisiana and combine forces with him for another attempt to take Shreveport.[12]

According to a staff officer, Steele considered Banks' proposal so absurd that he did not "entertain it for a moment." But he did reply, pointing out that the Confederates in Arkansas were reported to be receiving reinforcements and that he expected to be attacked, adding that: "The rebels are said to be much encouraged by an order of General E. K. Smith, detailing his successes against your command."[13] Steele also telegraphed summaries of all this to General Halleck, in this way becoming among the first to inform Washington of the collapse of the Union's drive in Louisiana.[14]

From all appearances, Frederick Steele simply did not know what to do. With Banks stalled the better part of a hundred miles south of Shreveport there was no point in pressing on in that direction. Sterling Price had enough cavalry to cut the escape route to Little Rock and to intercept supplies destined for Camden. How soon would the threat of starvation compel him to retreat? Or did honor require him to remain there and give battle when the reinforced Confederates approached?

N

Arkansas River

Saline River

Little Rock

Ouachita River

Jenkins' Ferry

Pine Bluff

Arkadelphia

Princeton

Washington

Marks' Mills

Poison Spring

Camden

Arkansas Battle Area

In the same order that General Halleck wrote regarding the change in command in Louisiana, he directed General Steele to return to Little Rock.[15] Frederick Steele received telegrams from Washington much faster than Banks, but Halleck's message had not even been written when adversity forced the commander of the federal forces in Arkansas to make a decision. Coping with shortages of food and fodder had been difficult enough; losing almost two hundred loaded wagons to the Confederates who whipped the federal escort at Poison Spring had made a bad situation much worse; and now, with Camden under siege, Steele's chances of continuing the campaign were hovering somewhere between zero and none at all.

All General Steele could claim with assurance in the way of achievement was that he had avoided being destroyed by Price, Marmaduke, and their cohorts. Actually his advance toward Shreveport had caused Edmund Kirby Smith to weaken Dick Taylor's combat power drastically enough to make inevitable Banks' escape from the island formed by the Cane and the Red Rivers. But the threat of starvation, and not mere awareness of the progress Kirby Smith was making on his way to reinforce Sterling Price, was uppermost in Fred Steele's mind. And this is why he was pitifully vulnerable to despair when he received the heart-stopping news of what had happened northeast of Camden at a place called Marks' Mills.

Earlier, a supply train from Pine Bluff had provided some temporary relief to the hunger pangs from which roughly ten thousand men and nine thousand horses and mules within Camden were suffering. Obviously, the next thing to do was to send the train back to Pine Bluff for more food and fodder.

On Friday, April 22, as Nathaniel Banks was abandoning Grand Ecore and Natchitoches and beginning his retreat to Alexandria, Steele sent the wagons back toward Pine Bluff. Also, to reduce the number of mouths to feed in Camden, he added sutlers, about three hundred freed slaves, cotton speculators, and other noncombatants to the procession. It was escorted by a force of near 1,440 soldiers, of which about 240 were cavalry; Lieutenant Colonel Francis M. Drake was its commander.[16]

Drake's column had been moving eastward along the Camden-Mount Elba road for two days when Confederate Brigadier General James F. Fagan, who had lived in that part of Arkansas and knew it well, was told by scouts that the Yankee wagons and their guards were headed for Pine Bluff. A little earlier General Kirby Smith, newly arrived near Camden and apparently irritated by Sterling Price's lethargy in carrying out an order the Trans-Mississippi Department's commander had given him, had sent Fagan north and east of Camden to sever Steele's lines of communication with Little Rock, Pine Bluff, and any other federally occupied sources of supplies. And so it was that James Fagan's cavalrymen were waiting on the morning of Monday, April 25, near Marks' Mills—several miles west of Mount Elba and the Saline River which the road to Pine Bluff crossed there.[17]

General Fagan had the luxury of several cavalry brigades to commit to the Yankees' annihilation. Not being learned in the military arts, Fagan sent his elements against the train and its defenders in a piecemeal fashion that prevented his assaults from having maximum destructive effect and resulted in his suffering heavier casualties than he might have had he given more care to executing what was essentially an ambush. Even so, his men captured all of the wagons the federals were unable to burn and took most of the survivors of his attack prisoners.[18]

Marks' Mills, as the fight came to be called, was one of those engagements that would be significant for reasons beyond the military outcome. This was the second time General Steele had sent out an escorted wagon train and again Confederate cavalry had destroyed it.

After this fresh disaster Steele did not see how he could remain at Camden. Even if Kirby Smith's force did not put the federal garrison to the sword during a climactic assault, after only a few days of siege men and animals would be dying of starvation and Steele would be obliged to surrender: Arkansas would revert to Confederate control and become the base for campaigns to drive Union forces from Missouri.

On the night of Monday, April 25, Fred Steele convened a council of war. His subordinates agreed that retreat was the only possible course of action, their differences being the point to which the army ought to fall back. Steele settled that matter quickly: Little Rock would be their destination.[19]

Two days later, in Washington, acting on behalf of the general-in-chief, Chief of Staff Henry Halleck would send the order telling General Steele to do what he had already decided—for reasons of his own—to do.[20]

+===+

At Camden on Tuesday, April 26, Frederick Steele and his subordinates supervised the destruction of everything of value that could not be loaded in the wagons remaining. Having in mind the prospect that many if not most of his starving animals would die along the way, a number of items—tents and even cooking utensils, to cite only two categories—were consigned to the flames, along with the better part of a hundred wagons. In their zeal to travel light the federal officers also burned bacon and hardtack that might have been given to the troops, each of whom would have no more than a half a pint of corn meal and a couple of crackers to last for however many days it would take them to march nearly a hundred and twenty miles.[21]

On that Tuesday night General Steele's drummers deceived the rebels besieging Camden by sounding the usual bedding-down signals. Toward midnight the last of the federals followed the wagon trains eastward across a pontoon bridge over the Ouachita River. Prudent if not also prescient, the rear guard then took up the bridge and escorted the wagons bearing it toward the other rivers Steele's army would have to cross before it reached Little Rock.[22]

Confederate General Edmund Kirby Smith, commander of the abbreviated siege of Camden, had denied Dick Taylor the use of the pontoon bridge he had kept at Shreveport, where the need for it in that location had long been a mystery. Lacking that resource, both of the cavalry thrusts General Taylor had thrown eastward after Pleasant Hill to trap David Dixon Porter's flotilla on the Red River had failed, the delay en route in crossing a flooded bayou becoming a partial cause of—among other things regrettable—the seasoned and highly respected Major General Tom Green's having his head blown off (as Admiral Porter put it in his report) by a gunboat's canister round during the fight at Blair's Landing.[23]

Yet Kirby Smith, in his haste to smite Steele hip and thigh, had neglected to bring his pontoon bridge along with him. Consequently, the general commanding the Confederate Department of the Trans-Mississippi was obliged to spend the whole day on Wednesday, April 27 in Camden, unable to pursue the retreating Yankees, watching his men improvise a bridge over the Ouachita.[24]

On the way from Shreveport to Camden Kirby Smith had kept in contact with his department's headquarters by telegraph, so he was aware of Taylor's reports of Nathaniel Banks' retreat from Grand Ecore to Alexandria and of Admiral Porter's plight. Taylor had never been reconciled to Kirby Smith's having taken his infantry divisions to Arkansas, and he both reiterated his request for their return and vented his anger again on April 28 in a long letter to the general commanding.

Kirby Smith's strategy, wrote Taylor from near Alexandria, was "fatally wrong" because it had abandoned "the certain destruction of an army of 30,000 men, backed by a huge fleet, to chase after a force of 10,000 in full retreat with over 100 miles start." Taylor continued:

> General, had you [after Pleasant Hill] *left the conduct of operations in my hands Banks' army would have been destroyed before this; the fleet would have been in our hands or blown up by the enemy. The moral effect at the*

North and the shock to public credit would have seriously affected the war. By this time the little division of Polignac and Vincent's Louisiana Cavalry would have been near the gates of New Orleans, prepared to confine the enemy to narrow limits. I would have been on my way with the bulk of my army to join Price at Camden, enriched with the captured spoils of a great army and fleet. Steele would have been brushed from our path as a cobweb before the broom of a housemaid; we would have reached St. Louis, our objective point, by midsummer and relieved the pressure from our suffering brethren in Virginia and Georgia. All this is as true as the living God and required no more than ordinary energy for its accomplishment . . .[25]

Promotion to lieutenant general would be acceptable, Taylor told Kirby Smith, if it were done by President Davis. It was, he said, "the duty of a soldier so to conduct himself as to dignify titles and not derive importance from them." He was discouraged and wished to be relieved of further duty under Kirby Smith's command.[26]

Earlier, Kirby Smith had wired Taylor that whipping Steele was still more important than completing Banks' destruction. He had backed that belief by ordering John Walker's division—formerly a part of Taylor's force, then being held at a midway location (so that Walker could rejoin Taylor quickly if Steele retreated)—to join Price's troopers at Camden. At about the same time, inexplicably, Kirby Smith sent Brigadier General Samuel B. Maxey and the units he had brought eastward back to the Indian Territory.[27] If Dick Taylor was both bewildered and embittered, then, by his superior's ordering up the Texans while sending away brigades already at Camden, it was certainly understandable.

Fully as baffling was Kirby Smith's decision to take his entire army and pursue Steele, knowing as he did from the many smoldering fires the federals had left behind that they were in deep trouble and from scouts' assurances that the retreating Yankees would find little or no food or forage in the barren country between Camden and Little Rock. But chase Steele he did, driving his men northward in heavy rainstorms that turned the roads into quagmires.

⊹⊱──⊰⊹

It was ironic that while Nathaniel Banks' forces were struggling with a river that was almost dry, Frederick Steele's men were having to search for a suitable place for crossing the flooded Saline. The overflow in Arkansas plagued both sides but it penalized the federals in particular. Roads turned into mud pools by spring rains slowed Steele's men, mules, and wagons, consuming precious time as well as energy. Discouraged soldiers threw away almost everything but their weapons, their ammunition, and such rations as they had left. Fear slogged with them, for Fagan's cavalry was rumored to be between them and Little Rock.[28]

The rumors were true but somewhat misleading. Kirby Smith had ordered James Fagan to get beyond the Saline and occupy a blocking position that would serve as an anvil when the Smith-led divisions caught up with Steele and hammered the Yankee troops against it. High water in the Saline obliged Fagan to keep moving northward through the river's soggy bottoms. When he did cross to the Little Rock side he was too far upstream to threaten the fugitives.[29] But Fred Steele's weary, hungry men did not know that on Friday, April 29, when they halted at Jenkins' Ferry on the Saline and their general ordered them to throw the pontoon bridge across the roaring stream.

Hastening the Union army's engineers' progress were reports that Kirby Smith's Confederates were near enough to attack at any time. By late afternoon on that Friday, though, the pontoon bridge was in place and the task of moving the wagon trains and artillery across the Saline began.[30] But rain and mud almost rendered their efforts futile. Reported Captain Junius Wheeler afterward:

> *Wagons settled to the axles and mules floundered about without a resting place for their feet. Fires were made along the road, pioneers and working details set to work, and every exertion was made to push the impediments across before daylight, it being evident that the enemy were in force in our rear. But we failed.*[31]

Torrential rain put out the fires, Wheeler wrote, "and the men became exhausted, and both they and the animals sank down in the mud and mire, wherever they were, to seek a few hours' repose."[32]

Nine miles to the southwest, near Princeton, the same rain was making the night miserable for Kirby Smith's infantrymen. Around midnight Thomas Churchill's division moved on toward Jenkins' Ferry, apparently on the theory that agony was easier to endure up and marching than while lying in muck. Not long after daylight the Confederates came to the rear of the line along which John Marmaduke's cavalrymen were pressing Steele's rear guard.[33]

Hardly anyone, least of all General Kirby Smith, had ever seen the terrain between Princeton and Jenkins' Ferry; if any of the rebels had, no doubt they would have advised the general commanding against picking a fight in what might well turn into a death trap. From about two miles southwest of the pontoon bridge the federals had thrown over the swollen Saline, the road from Camden and Princeton declined gradually into a narrow cul-de-sac formed by bluffs on either side. Down near the river were more features suggesting that the defenders had all of the advantages. To the left of the road was a bayou, with a cane swamp beyond it. On the right two cleared fields were separated by a grove of trees. Stands of timber lined the river and the high ground on both sides of the cul-de-sac.[34]

Frederick Steele, seasoned soldier than he was, made the most of nature's gift. By early morning he had his wagons and all but one of his artillery batteries on the Little Rock side of the Saline; also, he had used another boon—time gained because mud delayed the Confederates' advance—by having his infantrymen cut down trees along the river and use their trunks for barricades. His gunners could pour enfilade fire along Kirby Smith's columns as they advanced. And the volleys fired by Steele's federal foot soldiers from behind their improvised fortifications could cut down any rebels who survived his artillery's blasting. Kirby Smith would naturally try to find Steele's flanks. But timber thickets protected the Union line's eastern end and the bayou and swamp to the north of the road precluded such maneuvering.[35]

In these circumstances, the only course of action that might have saved Edmund Kirby Smith's army from a most glorious flogging would have been withdrawal back toward Camden. But he did no such thing. Instead, he threw in Churchill's division, committing one brigade after another, watching through the rain and battlesmoke as each in turn got shredded by the Yankee artillery and the stabbing fire of federal infantrymen behind their treetrunks.[36]

After more than two hours of witnessing nothing but the slaughter of Churchill's men Kirby Smith marked the arrival of Mosby Parsons' division by sending it down the lethal funnel to form on Churchill's right—not so much to try to get around Steele's eastern flank as to hold back the much-encouraged if half-starved veterans of Fred Steele's guided tour of central Arkansas. But exhaustion from long and hard marching on muddy roads, together with the appalling toll being taken by federal shell bursts and thick showers of minié balls, had weakened the Confederates too much for them to hold such ground as they had gained.

Having wasted the combat power of two divisions by feeding them in piecemeal, Kirby Smith compounded his manifold earlier blunders by sending in, one by one, the newly arrived but road-weary brigades of John Walker's division. Amid the wreckage of the units that had preceded them and the actual fog of warfare as savage as any ever seen anywhere west of the Mississippi, the Texans bought time in which the architect of this hid-

Jenkins' Ferry

eously costly debacle could think his situation through and decide what to do next.[37]

All General Steele had to do, as it turned out, was wait until Kirby Smith realized that his battered troops could do no more and ordered them to break contact and withdraw. Steele's patience was rewarded at a little after noon when the remnants of three Confederate divisions began drifting back up the road. In another hour or so all of the federals were on the northern bank of the Saline and the pontoon bridge was being dismantled.[38]

If Kirby Smith sought comfort in the expectation that James Fagan and his cavalrymen were somewhere between the far side of the Saline and Little Rock and that they might hold Steele until the rest of the Confederate army could strike it again, surely he was disappointed to see the riders arrive on the road from Princeton after the fighting was over. Fagan's force was the only one fresh enough to pursue the Yankees but it was on the wrong side of the Saline and Kirby Smith's pontoon bridge was in faraway Shreveport.[39]

For a time, though, it seemed that Steele's soldiers had emerged from the perils of battle only to become mired in the bottomless mud of the Saline's bottoms until starvation ended their ordeal. Runoffs from the recent rains made corduroying nigh-impossible. Horses and mules tugging wagons hub-deep in the wallows died in the traces. But with no rebel cavalry to harass them, the federals kept slogging through the waist-deep overflow toward high ground and—they hoped—Little Rock.[40]

⊹══⊹

Nathaniel Banks had made more than his share of mistakes, but now it seemed that Edmund Kirby Smith had been engaged in a perverse sort of contest with him to determine which of them could commit the most errors—or to see whose disasters would prove the most expensive. Banks' opportunities to mismanage were severely limited, at least for the time being, by being confined to Alexandria by the almost-dry Red River and Dick Taylor's small bands of gunners and cavalry. Kirby Smith's woes, however, were mostly self-inflicted.

Losses of perhaps a thousand of the eight thousand men Kirby Smith sent into the withering fire of Frederick Steele's four thousand effectives at Jenkins' Ferry accomplished precisely nothing, except the addition of perhaps 750 names to federal casualty lists. His piecemeal commitment of exhausted troops as soon as they came on the scene was as reprehensible as Major General George B. McClellan's overindulgence in that sin at

Antietam Creek back in September 1862. Kirby Smith's negligence in leaving his pontoon bridge behind precluded him from pursuing Steele's Yankees, imposing a cost to his reputation at least as high as that of his earlier failure to release the vital resource to Dick Taylor. Spooked by false rumors that the federals in Missouri were about to invade the Indian Territories, Kirby Smith sent General Maxey and his brigades westward, on April 27, at the very time he was in greatest need of cavalry in order to complete the annihilation of Steele's forces. But the most grievous blunder the commander of the Trans-Mississippi Department committed was his arrogant refusal to heed Taylor's warning that giving preference to mauling Steele's retreating force and letting Banks' army and David Dixon Porter's fleet escape destruction at or above Grand Ecore was insanity compounded.

More than a decade after the war ended, Richard Taylor's deep contempt for his superior's fatally flawed judgments was reflected in bitter, unforgiving words: "From first to last," he wrote, "General Kirby Smith seemed determined to throw a protecting shield around [Banks'] Federal army and fleet." And his scathing indictment continued:

> *In all the ages since the establishment of the Assyrian monarchy no commander has possessed equal power to destroy a cause. Far away from the great centers of conflict in Virginia and Georgia, on a remote theatre, the opportunity of striking a blow decisive of the war was afforded. An army that included the strength of every garrison from Memphis to the Gulf had been routed, and, by the incompetency of its commander, was utterly demoralized and ripe for destruction. But this army was permitted to escape . . . Vain indeed were our hopes. The commander of the "Trans-Mississippi" department had the power to destroy the last hopes of the Confederate cause, and exercised it with all the success of Bazaine at Metz.*[41]

+≡≡≡+

Not so eloquent was Ulysses Grant's reaction to General Banks' combination of misfeasance and malfeasance. All the general-in-chief wanted was the Bobbin Boy's scalp, or so he indicated in messages to Halleck in Washington. On May 3 Old Brains advised Grant:

> *I think the President will consent to the order if you insist on General Banks' removal as a military necessity, but he will do so very reluctantly, as it would give offense to many of his friends, and would probably be op-*

posed by a portion of his cabinet. Moreover, what could be done with Banks? He has many political friends who would probably demand for him a command equal to the one he now has.[42]

And who might be selected to replace Banks? "If you could go in person," wrote Grant to Halleck, "I believe it would be the best that could be done."[43] It certainly would have been an interesting solution, given Halleck's advocacy, as far back as November 1862, of the Red River as the proper line of operations for invading Texas. General Halleck replied that he would serve wherever Grant and Secretary of War Edwin Stanton thought best, but his own view was that he should remain in Washington in his present assignment.[44]

But the still-new general-in-chief seemed to have missed the warning regarding relieving Banks that Halleck had attempted to convey earlier; another demand that Banks be sacked drew from Halleck this sound, if somewhat schoolmasterish, reply:

General Banks is a personal friend of the President, and has strong political supporters in and out of Congress. There will undoubtedly be a very strong opposition to his being removed or superseded . . . To do an act which will give offense to a large number of his political friends the President will require some evidence in a positive form to show the military necessities of that act. In other words he must have something in a definite shape to fall back upon as his justification. You will perceive that the press in New Orleans and in the Eastern States are already beginning to open in General Banks' favor. The administration would be immediately attacked for his removal. Do not understand me as advocating his retention in command. On the contrary, I expressed to the President months ago my own opinion of General Banks' want of military capacity.[45]

General Halleck had been even more candid in a letter to General Sherman: "It seems but little better than murder to give important commands to such men as Banks, Butler, McClernand, Sigel, and Lew Wallace, and yet it seems impossible to prevent it."[46]

Orders placing Banks' second in command in charge of all military operations were thought by officials in the War Department to be on their way from Washington to Alexandria, but they would not reach their destination: an odd circumstance that would never be explained. General Grant had told Halleck that he had little confidence in William Franklin, whose record in the eastern battles had not been impressive.[47] But Franklin had departed Alexandria for New Orleans to have his leg (wounded at Sabine Crossroads) treated, so the general-in-chief's grudging approval no longer mattered.

Unlike his federal opposite number, General Kirby Smith was in no trouble with his superiors in his government's capital. "Success is a duty" was Nathaniel Banks' motto but Kirby Smith seemed to have borrowed it, for his report on the battle at Jenkins' Ferry reflected the same fact-warping that characterized Banks' conversions of his defeats into personal triumphs. "Your victories have caused the liveliest relief and rejoicing throughout the Confederacy," Secretary of War James A. Seddon wrote Kirby Smith after the mauling given his troops by Steele's, "and have riveted you, your gallant generals, and heroic soldiers in the gratitude and affection of the people. I congratulate you and them most heartily on the glorious results, and trust that the invaders have now been effectively punished and driven from the soil of the Trans-Mississippi Department."[48] President Davis offered similar effusions, adding substance to Richard Taylor's belief that the general commanding—or his "confidential staff"—had deliberately tampered with the truth.

While in Shreveport, Taylor wrote Kirby Smith, "I heard it announced that the signal victories at Mansfield and Pleasant Hill were triumphs of your skill and strategy—victories which your communications to me show you to have had as little connection as with the 'army in Flanders.' "[49] Rage probably caused Taylor to misremember Pleasant Hill, but he may have been correct in suspecting that Doctor Sol A. Smith, Kirby Smith's surgeon-general at Shreveport, had more than a little to do not only with decisions that proved counterproductive but with reports distorting their actual results.[50] Sol Smith's detestation of Taylor was matched only by his adoration of Kirby Smith, some said, and it was perhaps significant that the department commander wrote President Davis after Jenkins' Ferry to ask that Sol Smith be commissioned a brigadier general and named chief of staff, replacing Brigadier General William R. Boggs. Davis took no action on the request, by coincidence mirroring Abraham Lincoln's lack of interest in doing away with Nathaniel Banks.[51]

CHAPTER 7

REGATTA AT ALEXANDRIA

Clearly, the Union's Red River campaign was snakebit.

Major General Nathaniel P. Banks had been "gloriously flogged" by a Confederate force never stronger than half the number of troops in his own. Soon, with or without Rear Admiral David Dixon Porter's gunboats, Banks would have to abandon even Alexandria, the expedition's last base on the Red River. In Arkansas Major General Steele had been fortunate in saving his half-starved army from annihilation on its way back to Little Rock.

In Washington, President Abraham Lincoln and Major General Halleck were discovering that extricating federal forces from situations that could and probably would lead to imminent destruction presented much more complex challenges than those they had faced in launching the campaigns. Banks' attempts to establish a federal military presence in Texas had not prevented the French from continuing their efforts to make Mexico a part of Napoleon III's empire. Very few bales of Confederate cotton, other than those Porter's sailors had seized as "prizes of war," had reached the textile mills still operating in New England. And Lincoln could hardly expect his plan for restoration of the seceded states to be taken seriously with Union forces having to give major portions of Louisiana and Arkansas back to the rebels.

Nathaniel Banks' ineptitude had caused General-in-Chief Ulysses Grant to cancel his plans for the Mobile campaign, earlier an important element in his strategy for winning the war in 1864.[1] Similarly, Major General William T. Sherman was obliged to open his Atlanta drive without the ten thousand men Banks had borrowed but could not return. General Halleck had already lost most of his military reputation, but what was left of it seemed certain of being badly eroded because of his having been so persistent in his advocacy of entering East Texas by the Shreveport gateway.

How much blame should be assigned to General Banks' inadequacies, or to Richard Taylor's brilliance and perseverance, or to the pro-Confederate Red River's damp sand would be debated for decades by the fiasco's survivors and their posterity. But as April 1864 turned into May, the attention

125

of everyone concerned was focused on the low water at Alexandria that had trapped the navy's *Carondelet*, *Chillicothe*, *Lexington*, *Osage*, *Fort Hindman*, *Mound City*, *Neosho*, *Pittsburg*, *Ozark*, and *Louisville*.

The *Carondelet* would be especially hard to sacrifice. This gunboat with the melodic name was a veteran of almost all the navy's campaigns on western waters. Her first engagement, less than six months after she was launched, was in February 1862 in support of then-Brigadier General Grant's attacks aimed at capturing Fort Donelson on the Cumberland River. Gunners in the Confederates' shore batteries almost blew her out of the water. "Before the decks were well sanded," wrote her captain, Henry Walke, "there was so much blood on them that our men could not work the guns without slipping."[2] And at the time, the battered *Carondelet* was providing fire to cover withdrawal of the *Pittsburg* and *Louisville*, sisters again with her in adversity. Walke again risked the *Carondelet's* destruction two months later by running her past rebel batteries on Island No. 10 in the Mississippi one night during a fierce thunderstorm, proving that passage was possible and aiding greatly in the subsequent capture of that obstacle. She performed a similar role at Vicksburg as part of David Dixon Porter's flotilla assisting Ulysses Grant in the elimination of the last segment of Confederate control over the Big Muddy.[3]

But the *Carondelet's* greatest service had been rendered by her armament: three nine-inch Dahlgrens forward, two eight-inch guns, a hundred-pounder Parrott rifle on each of her beams, and two lighter Parrotts aft. Now the combined weight of all this ordnance, plus her iron plates, made the *Carondelet* a prime candidate for merciful scuttling, if water deep enough for that sad purpose could be found upstream.[4]

And much the same could have been said for the *Mound City*, *Chillicothe*, *Pittsburg*, *Ozark*, and *Louisville*.

Curiously, until the very end of April no one appeared to have given any consideration to an utterly brilliant suggestion Lieutenant Colonel Joseph Bailey had made weeks earlier to General Franklin, under whom the Wisconsin logger was serving as chief engineer. Anticipating that getting below the rapids down at Alexandria was going to be a major problem for Admiral Porter, on April 9—the day on which the battle of Pleasant Hill was fought—Bailey had shared with Franklin his idea of placing wing dams in the Red River above the falls, raising the water level and channeling the current through the gap in the center where the depth would be sufficient for any stranded gunboats to escape.[5]

During the siege of Port Hudson in 1863 Colonel Bailey had applied his experience as a timberman by building log dams in the Mississippi to raise the water level in the vicinity of the sunken Confederate steamboats

USS *Carondelet*

Starlight and *Red Chief* enough to float them. But on that April day when Bailey had first made his proposal Franklin's mind had been on the more immediate challenge the advance of Dick Taylor's forces was posing. Now the potential disaster had developed into a very real one, yet no one showed any interest when Bailey advanced his idea again. Even Admiral Porter, presumably the man whose desire to save the fleet was greatest, was skeptical. "If damning would get the fleet off," he quipped, "I would have been steaming down the river long before."[6]

General Franklin encouraged Bailey to make one more attempt to persuade Banks to approve the project. Some effort to float the navy's trapped ironclads *had* to be made; otherwise, it would appear to the Northern public that Banks had been indifferent, even grossly negligent. "We have more to fear from our friends," Banks had said back at Strasburg two years earlier, "than from the bayonets of our enemies," and evidently he realized that this was more true than ever as April was turning into May in 1864. In any case, he finally adopted Bailey's plan to build wing and tree dams above the Red River's falls and provided five thousand troops to carry it out.

Work began on Saturday, April 30. Years later, Colonel James G. Wilson described the scene at Alexandria as the men from northwestern states' regiments got busy:

> There were also employed in the construction of this great work some two hundred army wagons and about a thousand horses, mules, and oxen. Several hundred hardy lumbermen, belonging to a regiment from Maine, were employed on the left, or north, bank in felling trees, while an equal number were engaged in hauling them to the river bank. Flat-boats were constructed, on which stone was brought from above, after being quarried, and the work was begun at the foot of the falls by running out a tree-dam made from heavy timber and stone, crosstied with the trunks of other large trees, and strengthened in every way which Yankee ingenuity could devise. This dam extended out into the river a distance of above three hundred feet. Four large navy coal barges were then filled with stone and brick, and sunk at the end of the dam. From the right, or south, bank—there being no timber there—a series of heavy cribs were constructed from material obtained by demolishing some old mills and barns, while the brick, iron, and stone required to sink them and hold them in their place, were procured by tearing down two large sugar houses, and by taking up a quantity of railroad iron, buried in the vicinity of Alexandria. In this work several hundred colored troops were employed, while the white troops carried forward the operations on the other side of the river, both details working day and night.[7]

Until the work had been in progress for a week, Wilson recalled, "not ten percent of the officers and seamen of the navy had the slightest faith in our saving their fleet." Admiral Porter gave the project only scant attention. Banks, however, rode out frequently to inspect the dam and cribs Bailey and his crews were building.[8]

General Banks had nothing much to fear from Confederates, due mainly to Kirby Smith's having taken the greater part of Dick Taylor's little army on the Arkansas glory hunt, but he had the Alexandria area converted into a fort anyway. Two lines of trenches, gun emplacements, and obstacles protected the town and the dam site. Reinforcements arrived from the abandoned Texas beachheads. Soon Banks' forces numbered more than thirty-one thousand and he had eighty guns, all devoted to keeping Porter's vessels from being captured by less than five thousand rebels.[9]

About all Taylor could do with so few men was threaten the defenders. Brigadier General Liddell, commanding a small force on the Red River's northeastern bank, was able to get within artillery range of Bailey's operations but he had no guns and Taylor had no way of getting any to him. Thirty miles below Alexandria, however, at a place called David's Ferry, Taylor's audacity in splitting such strength as he had gave Confederate spirits a momentary boost.

Brigadier General James Major's cavalry, supported by a battery of artillery, captured the federal transport *Emma* and burned her. That was on May 1. Three days later the *City Belle* steamed upstream into an ambush that deprived Banks of the vessel and seven hundred reinforcements destined for his army. Nearer Alexandria on that day, moving downstream with a regiment of furlough-bound Ohio soldiers on board, the transport *John Warner* came under attack but kept going, helped through one danger zone by two tinclads escorting her; the next morning, though, her luck ran out. Wrote George P. Lord, who had the curious title of acting volunteer lieutenant, master of the tinclad Covington:

At Dunn's Bayou (on the right, going down) we were fired upon by two pieces of artillery and infantry. The Covington *was hit by this battery only three times, and the* Warner's *rudders were disabled, but she still continued downstream until she came to a short point in the river, when she went into the bank. She had no sooner struck the bank when a rebel battery on the right shore going down, and from 4,000 to 5,000 infantry, opened on her and my vessel.*[10]

So Lord reported; but in fact, George Baylor had about a thousand cavalrymen and four artillery pieces.[11] Later, in his report to Secretary of the Navy Welles, Porter raised Baylor's troop strength to six thousand accompanied by twenty-five guns.[12] But Lord's account continued:

> Almost every shot either stuck the boilers, steam pipe, or machinery of the Warner, as she was only about 100 yards from the battery. After we had engaged the battery about three hours the Warner hoisted a white flag. We still kept up our fire, and I sent a party from my vessel under a severe fire to burn her, but the colonel in charge sent me word that there were nearly 125 killed and wounded, and requested that I would not burn her, which was granted.[13]

Next, Lord's *Covington* tried to assist the other tinclad, the *Signal*, which presented the Confederates with the spectacle of three Yankee boats disabled, two of them adrift, the other captured. "Finding it impossible to handle my vessel," wrote Lord, "and fearing I should get on the side where artillery and infantry were, I went over on the other bank and made fast, head upstream."[14]

But Lord and his men on the *Covington* fought on:

> I used my stern guns on the lower battery and my broadside on the infantry abreast of us and my bow guns on the battery that was ahead of us, which had been brought down from Dunn's Bayou.
>
> My escape pipe was cut while alongside the Signal, causing a great deal of steam to escape and making the impression that the boilers had been struck; however, the men rallied and kept up a brisk fire on the enemy . . .
>
> My ammunition gave out, my howitzers were all disabled by the bracket bolts drawing out, and every shot coming through us. With one officer and a good many of my men already killed, I determined to burn my vessel. I spiked the guns, had coals of fire strewn on the deck, and myself and the executive officer set fire to the cotton, which was on the guards alongside of the engine. I saw it burning finely before I left, and feel sure she was destroyed.[15]

On the bank opposite the rebels, Acting Lieutenant Lord collected his survivors: nine of his original fourteen officers, but only twenty-three of the sixty-two men in his crew when he had left Alexandria. Lord led his depleted force toward that town, but before midnight the group was dispersed by Confederate cavalry. But four days later, when he wrote his report to Porter, he was able to conclude: "I am glad to say that they have nearly all arrived here safely."[16]

Such details were welcome, for now the admiral faced the understandably difficult task of informing Gideon Welles that in the space of a few days, small bands of Confederates had destroyed or captured two gunboats and three transports, inflicting in the process close to six hundred casualties without suffering any losses themselves. Porter would not disclose, however, that the Confederates had also closed the Red River as a federal line of communication between Alexandria and New Orleans.

+==+

Interest in events transpiring west of the Mississippi was almost totally eclipsed early in May 1864 by the opening of General Grant's "overland" campaign west of Fredericksburg in Virginia, and concurrently the start of Sherman's advance toward rebel General Joseph E. Johnston's fortified positions on high ground in northwest Georgia called by Sherman "the terrible door of death." Missing from the list of end-the-war moves by Union armies was the drive toward Mobile Major General Banks would have been leading if only—well, later Senator Wade and his Radical-dominated Joint Congressional Committee on the Conduct of the War would try to determine why Banks was, instead, detained at Alexandria.

But as every combat veteran knows, all that really matters is what is happening in his immediate vicinity that may have bearing on his own future. And so the most important change taking place anywhere in the war was, to the soldiers and especially the sailors isolated at Alexandria, the rise in the Red River's water level.

For more than a week several thousand men had been at work around the clock (in the words of Colonel Wilson) "moving heavy logs to the outer end of the tree dam, throwing in brushwood and branches of trees to make it tight, wheeling bricks out to the cribs, carrying bars of railway iron to the barges, and in various other ways contributing to the work, while on each bank of the river were to be seen thousands of spectators, consisting of officers of both services, groups of sailors, soldiers, camp-followers, and citizens of Alexandria, all eagerly watching our progress and discussing the chances of success."[17]

As if to suggest that nothing was likely to come of this gargantuan effort, Admiral Porter issued no orders to lighten the trapped ironclads or to make any preparations for a run through the gap between the tree dam and the end of the line of cribs. When Colonel Wilson discovered that each of the deep-draft gunboats had bales of cotton stored in their holds, he went directly to General Banks. "I did not think we should be working there like beavers," he told the members of the Joint Congressional Committee on the Conduct of the War, "night and day, to construct a dam to float these vessels when they were loaded down with cotton."[18] Banks agreed; later, Porter told his crews to remove the bales, but the prizes of war were still aboard on May 8 when the water being backed up by the dam, cribs, and sunken barges in between had made the stretch below the upper falls deep enough for the ponderous ironclads to begin their trips either to freedom or destruction.[19]

On that Sunday the sight of high water excited General Banks so much he ordered his subordinates to be ready to start the march to New Orleans on two hours' notice and he even had the orders prepared designating the sequence of units in the column.[20] So indifferent were some of Porter's officers, however, that only the captains of the *Osage*, *Fort Hindman*, and *Neosho* took advantage of Colonel Bailey's apparent success by steaming past the upper falls into the pool the dam had created.[21]

At one o'clock on Monday morning Banks sent Porter a warning:

Colonel Bailey informs me that the water has risen upon the dam 2 feet since sundown and is still rising. It is impossible to say how long the dam may stand the effects of a continued rise. The pressure is terrific. The boats of the fleet ought to be put in readiness at once to take advantage of high water. I have been up to the fleet this morning, and found everything so quiet and still that I feared that there might be unnecessary delay in the movements in the morning, and ask your attention to it.[22]

Still before sunrise, the general wrote Porter again:

There is a space of 20 feet or more between the tree dam and the barge which, when filled, will raise the water from 6 to 10 inches, giving, we think, sufficient depth for the passage of the boats. Every exertion ought to be made to get them ready tonight, so that they may pass the falls to-morrow.

And as if to underscore the urgency of acting, Banks added:

I regret to say that our forage is so reduced that it will be impossible to remain here longer without imperiling the safety of the animals attached to the trains and the artillery. We have exhausted the country, and with the march that is before us it will be perilous to remain more than another day.[23]

But the pro-Confederate Red River did not wait for Admiral Porter to react to these messages. At around five o'clock on that Monday morning the pressure of impounded water swept away two of the large coal barges that had been sunk in the center of the river. Later, in a report to Secretary of the Navy Gideon Welles, Porter described what happened next:

Seeing this unfortunate accident, I jumped on a horse and rode to the point where the upper vessels were anchored, and ordered the Lexington to pass the upper falls, if possible, and immediately attempt to go through the [opening in the] dam . . . The Lexington succeeded in getting over the upper falls, just in time, the water rapidly falling as she was passing over. She then steered directly for the opening in the dam, through which the water was rushing so furiously that it seemed as if nothing but destruction awaited her. Thousands of beating hearts looked on anxious for the result; the silence was so great as the Lexington approached the dam that a pin might almost be heard to fall. She entered the gap with a full head of steam on, pitched down the roaring torrent, made two or three spasmodic rolls, hung for a moment on the rocks below, was then swept into deep water by the current and rounded to, safely into the bank.

Thirty thousand voices rose in one deafening cheer, and universal joy seemed to pervade the face of every man present.[24]

The *Neosho* followed, and then the *Fort Hindman* and the *Osage*. But the water level above the dam had fallen so rapidly and so far that the *Carondelet*, *Chillicothe*, *Mound City*, *Pittsburg*, *Ozark*, and *Louisville* appeared to be doomed.[25]

On one hand, it could be argued that Bailey's having saved four of Porter's ironclads was a victory of sorts—enough of one, anyway, to justify sacrificing the rest of the Mississippi River Squadron and leaving the wreckage and Alexandria to Dick Taylor. Such a course of action would at least ease Banks' embarrassment over having been held captive there for weeks not only by a pro-Confederate river but by a rebel force less than one-fifth the size of his own.

But Joe Bailey was not ready to give up. Rather than do any more to the present obstructions, he suggested building a series of wing dams at the head of the upper falls. Bailey's men, many of whom had been working night and day for over a week, were eager to give his idea a try.[26]

Belatedly, Admiral Porter ordered the removal of the guns, ammunition, stores, and iron plates from the gunboats still trapped above the upper falls. Bailey used the time gained to start building the tree dams upstream.

General Banks watched for two days, then sent Colonel Wilson to visit Porter, who was incapacitated by an ailment that he said "perfectly prostrates me when I ride on horseback or move about."[27] In a letter to Banks written after Wilson departed, the admiral responded to the impatient general's prodding:

> Colonel Wilson . . . seemed to think the navy were relaxing their exertions above [the falls] . . . Don't suppose because the vessels seem quiet that nothing is being done; everything is being done that can be. I hope you will look this matter patiently in the face. I am sure Colonel Bailey will have every vessel through in two days, and though you are pressed for forage, two days will really amount to almost nothing, and any loss we might sustain in horses up to that time would be nothing in comparison to the loss of one of those vessels.

Admiral Porter then turned to a subject he must have assumed would be much on Banks's mind: public opinion:

> If we have met with reverses above, the rescue of this fleet from its peculiar position will redeem the past. You must have seen the tendency of the Northern press to cavil at our movements out here, and they can not help but admit, if we succeed, that amidst our trouble, the best piece of engineering ever performed in the same space of time has been accomplished under difficulties the rebels deemed insurmountable. Now, general, I really see nothing that should make us despond . . . I hope, sir, you will not let anything divert you from the attempt to get these vessels all through safely, even if we have to stay here and eat mule meat.[28]

"We shall not leave this post until the vessels are released," General Banks replied. And he added: "Thus far the representations to the Northern press are most likely made by men who ran away from the scene of the action. When men fail to do their duty they are most anxious to justify it by partial representation of the facts."[29]

⊢━━⊣

David Dixon Porter, like Banks, was a master at reporting unpleasant events in words that would cause his superiors in Washington minimal upset. This skill may be discerned in the passage of his letter to Secretary Welles following his description of the *Lexington*'s successful trip over the falls on May 9:

The Neosho *followed next, all her hatches battened down and every pre-caution taken against accident. She did not fare as well as the* Lexington, *her pilot having become frightened as he approached the abyss, and stopped her engine, when I particularly ordered a full head of steam to be carried; the result was that for a moment her hull disappeared from sight under the water. Every one thought she was lost. She rose, however, swept along over the rocks with the current, and fortunately escaped with only one hole in her bottom, which was stopped in the course of an hour. The* Hindman *and* Osage *both came through beautifully without touching a thing, and I thought if I was only fortunate enough to get my large vessels as well over the falls, my fleet once more would do good service on the Mississippi . . . On the whole, it was very fortunate that the dam was carried away, as the two barges that were swept away from the center, swung around against some rocks on the left and made a fine cushion for the vessels, and pre-vented them, as it afterwards appeared, from running on certain destruc-tion.*[30]

While Colonel Bailey and his "noble-hearted soldiers" were repairing the damage, Porter was suffering from the "complaint that perfectly pros-trates me" he had mentioned earlier, but he assured Welles that he "knew every hour what is going on and give directions accordingly." Typical of the information he was receiving from his gunboats' captains was this mes-sage from Lieutenant Commander John G. Mitchell, the *Carondelet's* mas-ter:

I am getting spars in place and shall use them at once. Colonel Bailey will haul our stern out with a windlass from the right bank of the river. I would suggest that one of the other vessels drop down, if the Mound City gets through, until nearly the stern of this vessel, which will make dead water on our starboard quarter and enable us to haul the easier . . . We can go no further on the rocks, as I have run all the guns over on our port side to keep her from sliding up; this and the spars will hold us.[31]

And from Lieutenant Commander E. K. Owen on the *Louisville:*

The Mound City *has succeeded in getting abreast of the* Carondelet. *There is plenty of water all around her, but she appears to be aground somewhere about midships. The water is rising at the rate of 2 inches in six hours . . .*[32]

Later, from Commander Selfridge on the *Mound City*:

We started the Mound City *this forenoon a length and a half. We shall have her over all right, I hope, in the course of the afternoon. The* Carondelet *is all afloat only waiting for the former to get down. The channel is very lumpy, which makes the delay.*

Everything looks encouraging to get three of the "turtles" over before 8 P.M. Water still rising slowly.[33]

And again from Mitchell:

With regard to the statement of General Banks that we have done nothing during the night, I would simply state that we have been at work all night, and have succeeded in hauling her ahead 45 feet and are nearly across the lumps in the channel.

I have sent an order to the commanding officers of the Pittsburg *and* Mound City *to take position to throw water on the falls with their wheels and have an anchor planted on the other side of the lower shoal, which can be used by the boats in succession as they come on the falls.*[34]

On May 11 and 12 the six gunboats passed the upper falls. "A good deal of labor having been expended in hauling then through," wrote Porter to Secretary Welles, "the channel being very crooked, scarcely wide enough for them." On the following day all the vessels made it past the break in the dam. "By 3 o'clock that afternoon," the admiral reported, "the vessels were all coaled, ammunition replaced, and all steamed down the river, with the convoy of transports in company."[35]

Yet there was more to the story of how the federal gunboats escaped the equally undesirable fates of capture or destruction, and Porter passed it along on May 19 in a message to the secretary of the navy. As was his wont, the admiral placed emphasis on advantages embedded in apparent adversity:

In my report [dated May 16] in relation to the release of the gunboats from their unpleasant position above the falls I did not think it prudent to mention that I was obliged to destroy 11 32-pounders, not having time to haul them from above the falls to Alexandria, the army having moved and drawn in all their pickets. The 32-pounders were old guns and would have been condemned at the first opportunity.

For the same reasons I also omitted to mention that I was obliged to take off the iron from the sides of the Pook[36] gunboats and from the Ozark to get them over.

Not being able to haul this iron around the falls to Alexandria, for want of wagons, I ordered the gunboats to run up the river at night to a point where they could find 5 to 6 fathoms of water, where the iron was thrown overboard, and where, in a few moments, it would sink many feet under the quicksands, thus leaving no possible chance for the rebels to recover it.

The Pook vessels run so much better without this iron than they ever did before, and it never having been of any use to them, I propose leaving it off altogether. Their forward casemates are still heavily protected with iron, and as they always fight bow on, it is all they should carry. Besides, they are getting old, and having done a great deal of service without any repairs, they can not bear the weight. They now run 2 to 2 ½ knots faster than before . . .[37]

Admiral Porter was quite right in informing Welles that "The highest honors the Government can bestow on Colonel Bailey can never repay him for the service he has rendered the country."[38] The successful completion of what Porter had called "the best engineering feat ever performed" was marred however, by the shameless conduct of Union officers and men who burned Alexandria and by the hypocrisy and negligence of their army's commander.

Banks' preparations for abandoning Alexandria and statements made by some of his subordinates fed rumors to the effect that the town was going to be put to the torch. On May 9 and again on the thirteenth Banks gave alarmed citizens the impression that he had ordered a cavalry force of five hundred troopers to prevent "conflagration" and all other criminal acts; later, the officer to whom the instruction was said to have been given disavowed any knowledge of such a directive.[39] Moreover, fires were ignited in virtually all parts of the town at about the same moment; some Yankee soldiers carried buckets containing a mixture of turpentine and camphor and smeared it on houses and other buildings with mops.[40]

Wrote an eyewitness afterward:

There is no use trying to tell about the sights I saw and the sounds of distress I heard. It cannot be told and could hardly be believed if it were told. Crowds of people, men, women, children and soldiers, were running with all they could carry, when the heat would become unbearable, and dropping all, they would flee for their lives, leaving everything but their bodies to burn. Over the levee the sights and sounds were harrowing. Thousands of people, mostly women, children and old men, were wringing their hands as they stood by the little piles of what was left of all their worldly possessions. Thieves were everywhere, and some of them were soldiers.[41]

Residents of Alexandria who were Unionists suffered along with everyone else. Many who had helped Banks try to carry out Abraham Lincoln's program to restore Louisiana to statehood during late March and early April attempted to board transports bound for New Orleans, but they were rudely turned away.[42]

Initially, some of Banks' staff officers did all that they could to stop the spread of the wind-driven flames—in vain. The general commanding had already departed, leaving behind many victims of the atrocity who would question the assurances he had given them earlier but who were certain that Banks had done nothing to restrain Major General A. J. Smith and his arsonists.[43]

That was on May 13. The next afternoon Richard Taylor sent this terse message to Hydrocephalus at Shreveport:

The enemy left Alexandria after mid-day to-day, burning the place. Two houses only reported left between the ice house and railroad. Heavy fighting all day with gunboats and troops. [Brigadier General William] Steele's division in their rear; Polignac, Major, and Bagby in front and on flank; Harrison, reinforced by Likens' regiment, on north side of Red River. We have experienced some loss, but will continue to fight them to the bank of the Mississippi and beyond, if possible.[44]

+➤══◄+

During April Major General Banks' army had gained considerable experience in retreating, first from Pleasant Hill to Grand Ecore and then from there to Alexandria. Now, in mid-May, with Admiral Porter's gunboats saved and well downriver, the question facing Banks became one of how to get his army to the Mississippi River and out of harm's way.

This was no small challenge, despite the addition of troops who had returned from the abandoned beachheads along the Texas coast (more than replacing Banks' earlier losses), because only a small fraction of the total present for duty had been crammed onto the transports the gunboats escorted toward the Big Muddy. And Banks still labored under the delusion that Richard Taylor had upward of twenty-five thousand men ready to bedevil him.

In fact, the Confederates were outnumbered by about five to one, but of one thing the federal general commanding could be certain: Taylor had plenty of guns now, most of them captured at Sabine Crossroads.[45] Also, Banks, who had admitted two years earlier that he had "more to fear from our friends than the bayonets of our enemies," may have been mindful of what the war managers in Washington and the reporters for the Northern newspapers would think of him and say about him if Dick Taylor caught him in another murderous Sabine Crossroads-type trap.

But, as during Banks' skedaddle from Grand Ecore to Alexandria, Taylor suffered from the lack of enough men to drive Banks into the river and drown his army. Moreover, in the flat bayou-drained country into which the war had moved, Taylor had no terrain advantages (such as the narrow road through the tunnel formed by the pine forests south of Mansfield) to aid him in smiting the Yankees hip or thigh.[46]

General Banks' route toward the Mississippi had been blazed back in mid-March by A. J. Smith's marauders on their way northwestward from Simmesport. There being nothing much left to burn on the way back, Smith's command fell "into its old place in the rear" (as he put it in his report).[47] And as in the withdrawal from Grand Ecore to Alexandria, Banks placed William Emory's troops up front.[48]

By sundown on May 15 the retreating federals had reached Marksville, forty miles southeast of the suburb of Hell into which they had converted Alexandria. Thus far there had been only light skirmishing. Taylor was thinking ahead, however, as this excerpt from a message he sent on May 14 to Shreveport indicates:

> My troops are so disposed as to harass the enemy in rear and flank and attack the boats from both banks of the river. Having no frontier which offers advantage to a small force, I have not the pretension to attempt to fight a general battle with my little force against four times their number, with one flank resting on Red River supported by gun-boats; but I hope to force the enemy to destroy large amounts of property, and harass and worry him until he reaches the Mississippi. The troops from above cannot reach me in time to be of use in this campaign. I shall direct General Walker to halt at Campti and rest and reorganize his command. His presence here at the right time would have insured the most brilliant results; but such opportunities never occur twice in the same campaign. As soon as Banks reaches the Mississippi River he will lose the troops of the Sixteenth and Seventeenth Corps loaned him by Sherman. Even if he withdraws every man from Texas, which he will do, he cannot do more than maintain himself in New Orleans.[49]

On the next day, May 15, Taylor's troops slowed the federal advance.

"[William] Steele's division pressed the enemy's rear and flank on the river road," he wrote in a report dated May 16, "while Bagby's division, afterward re-enforced by Major, beat back several times the head of [Banks'] column as it attempted to *debouche* on the high ground of the Marksville Prairie from the Choctaw Swamp. Heavy loss was inflicted on the enemy, Bagby skillfully masking his artillery and using it at short range. Late in the evening the-enemy turned the position by bringing up his masses, and we fell back to Mansura, Marksville being occupied by him during the night."[50]

Mansura was important to Banks because the blocking position Taylor had established there covered three roads diverging south of the town, each leading to the last major stream his army would have to cross: Atchafalaya Bayou. "[Taylor] manifested a determination here to obstinately resist our passage," Banks said in his account of the ensuing fight.[51] So it must have seemed; here is how the Confederate put it:

At early dawn this morning skirmishing began along our line, of which Mansura was the center, Bagby and Major, with nineteen pieces of artillery, holding the right, and Polignac, re-enforced by two regiments of cavalry under Debray, the left, with thirteen pieces of artillery, including two 30-pounder Parrotts. The broad, open prairie, smooth as a billiard table, afforded an admirable field for artillery practice, and most of our guns were 3-inch rifle and 10-pounder Parrotts captured from the enemy. About 6 A.M. the action became general, the enemy bringing up masses of infantry with several batteries.[52]

In this open prairie country both armies got good looks at each other. A Yankee soldier later recalled "[troops] resplendent in steel and brass; miles of lines and columns; the cavalry gliding over the ground in the distance with a delicate, nimble lightness of innumerable twinkling feet; a few batteries enveloped in smoke and incessant thundering, others dashing swiftly to salient positions; division and corps commanders with their staff officers clustering about them, watching through their glasses the hostile army; couriers riding swiftly from wing to wing; everywhere the beautiful silken flags; and the scene ever changing with the involutions and evolutions of the host."[53]

Richard Taylor described some of those involutions and evolutions in his report:

Several attempts to turn our right were signally repulsed, as were the efforts to advance on our center. At 10 A.M. long lines of infantry commenced demonstrations on our left, the pivot of the position, our trains being behind that flank near Evergreen. This rendered the position dangerous, as the enemy had probably 16,000 men on the field, and perhaps more. Our men withdrew with the steadiness of veterans on parade, and the road to Simsport [sic] was left open to the foe. Our artillery was most admirably served, and told heavily on the long lines and heavy columns of the enemy, while our short, thin line offered a small mark.[54]

Mansura would remain mostly a picture-book battle, but an engagement fought near Yellow Bayou on May 17 and 18 proved more costly in both sides' casualties. Moreover, this was as messy an encounter as Mansura had been ultra-neat.

Confederate General Wharton opened the action by attacking Banks' rear; the federals ambushed Debray's cavalry, which then struck the flank of the Yankee force resisting Wharton; concurrently, another rebel unit was cutting into a Union wagon train but had to destroy it because A. J. Smith's rear guard filled the only road. Both sides fought with fury heightened by the fact that high water in the Mississippi had backed up into the Atchafalaya Bayou, broadening that stream—which General Banks' forces absolutely had to cross—to roughly six hundred yards. Southern victory would make it easier for Taylor to build a line confining the Yankees to the western bank of an apparently impassable waterway; survival was at stake for the invaders.

Flooding had raised the stakes, but nature employed another element that doomed the back-and-forth fighting at Yellow Bayou to a stalemate: Burning underbrush forced both sides to disengage. For Taylor's men the campaign was over, the last chance to smite their enemies drifting off with the smoke from the fires. Banks' federals were more fortunate. As at Pleasant Hill, A. J. Smith's troops had saved the Union army by attacking at Yellow Bayou in time to prevent the Confederates from disrupting a second miracle that was being wrought by Lieutenant Colonel Joseph Bailey.[55]

During March, April, and half of May, too little water coming down the Red River had plagued the Union expedition; now, too much of it separated Napoleon P. Banks' army from the Mississippi and the steamers assembled to transport A. J. Smith's troops belatedly to Memphis and the rest to sanctuary at New Orleans. However, the danger to the troops and the presence of all those boats made Bailey look upon them as oversize pontoons. Low on coal though many of them were, he had the vessels steam from wherever they had been into the Atchafalaya and anchor in a line across it. Using timber looted from the few buildings A. J. Smith's arsonists had overlooked on their arrival two months earlier, troops directed by Bailey built a bridge spanning the bayou. Wagons (and later, men) moved up the western ramp to the first ship's deck level and then down or up again, depending on the size of the next vessel serving as a pontoon, over and over until they reached the ramp leading to the dry land of the Mississippi's west bank.

Thanks to A. J. Smith's timely check of Confederate assaults at Yellow Bayou and Joe Bailey's brilliant improvisation, Major General Nathaniel P. Banks had survived—only to find Major General Edward R. S. Canby waiting on May 19 with orders from Washington relieving Banks of command.[56]

CHAPTER 8

AFTERWORDS

HEADQUARTERS, DISTRICT OF WEST LOUISIANA,
In the Field, May 18, 1864

* * *

The campaign will probably close to-day at Simsport [sic], its point of de-parture, after nearly seventy days of uninterrupted fighting. Nothing but the withdrawal of Walker's division from me has prevented the capture of Banks' army and the destruction of Porter's fleet. I feel bitterly about this, because my army has been robbed of the just measure of its glory and the country of the most brilliant and complete success of the war . . .[1]

So wrote Major General Richard Taylor to Trans-Mississippi Depart-ment headquarters at Shreveport as Union Major General Nathaniel Banks' forces were escaping over the bridge Lieutenant Colonel Joseph Bailey had improvised. The bitterness Taylor expressed, however, was mild compared with statements he made in messages he sent General Edmund Kirby Smith in the weeks to come. And acrimonious though these Confed-erates' disputes would become, their enemies seemed even more deter-mined to stretch the limits of vituperation.

Records on which posterity would have to rely suggest that the Union-initiated Red River Expedition was a man-made disaster that resembled natural ones such as hurricanes, vast forest fires, and prolonged drought. Virtually everyone drawn into it, or who was even remotely involved in it, lost. Ashes, graves, and ruined reputations were all that remained when the last Yankee soldier boarded the sole remaining New Orleans-bound transport waiting on the west bank of the Mississippi after Bailey's boat bridge over the flooded Atchafalaya had been dismantled.

Various witnesses testifying before Ben Wade's Joint Congressional Committee on the Conduct of the War gave a wide variety of answers to the question, why was this fiasco ever undertaken? None of those attempts really succeeded, mainly because the Red River Expedition of 1864 was a lesser included offense in a vastly larger felony: federal invasion of states Abraham Lincoln insisted had never left the Union. Put as kindly as may be possible, the tragedy along the river of damp sand was a by-product of the Washington war managers' desire to run a bluff against the French in Mexico, New England industrialists' lust for cotton, and a president's craving for a second term.

The story of *how* the expedition failed has just been told, and from that narrative posterity can draw conclusions as to *why* the campaign was such a disaster for both sides. In order to round out an analysis of these events, however, consider some of the consequences of failure that impacted the futures of the movers and shakers.

✦━━✦

First and perhaps foremost, Abraham Lincoln.

During 1861 and 1862 the North paid an appalling price for having elected a president utterly unqualified to act effectively as commander-in-chief in a war of unprecedented size, complexity, and ferocity.[2] By the fall of 1863, however, Confederate weakness and increased professionalism in the federal armies had given the Union victories that enabled Lincoln to cut back his direct involvement in military operations and to devote more of his attention to political and economic matters. Quelling the rebellion remained his main objective, but it was by no means clear that he could complete that task before the expiration of his term; he needed to be re-elected in November 1864, and this appeared to have been a factor in his effort to begin the "restoration" of some of the seceded states without waiting for the guns to cool. And among the most promising states for early re-admission, in his view, was Louisiana.

Whatever the trends in Lincoln's thinking may have been, his role in the Red River Expedition's gestation was more of a political or economic nature than military and he took no part in its conduct. Of course, as commander-in-chief he bore the ultimate responsibility for all failures. But in this one he may have been merely negligent; given his inability to whip Stonewall Jackson in the Shenandoah Valley Campaign back in 1862, it may have been just as well that he stood aside.

For reasons that surely seemed good and sufficient in the wake of Fort Sumter, an unqualified commander-in-chief had commissioned Nathaniel Banks, a politician who was equally unqualified, a major general—and a very high ranking one, at that. Thereafter, Banks did nothing but let Lincoln down. In a strict sense, all the damage Banks did after Stonewall Jackson sent him fleeing to Maryland in May 1862 can be charged to the

President for not having removed him permanently from command of combat forces on that shameful occasion.

However, after sending Banks to New Orleans the Union's President compounded the mistake of supporting him; to military duties beyond the general's capacity he added a complex political mission without precedent in its nature. Hindsight strongly suggests that the Red River Expedition ought to have been led by a soldier who could have cleared enough of Louisiana for Banks, acting in a purely political capacity, to devote his true talents and pre-war experience exclusively to preparing Louisiana for restoration—to set an example Lincoln could provide to a Congress in which Radical Republicans were bent on returning the South, when conquered, to the Stone Age.

The commander-in-chief committed much the same sin by requiring Major General Frederick Steele to do all toward Arkansas' restoration that he had charged Banks with achieving in Louisiana. In this instance Lincoln's judgment lapse was all the more to be regretted, for (unlike Banks) Fred Steele was a professional army officer to whom involvement in civilian politics had quite properly been discouraged by regular army tradition. Again, if Lincoln had sent down someone equipped to engineer the erring sister's return to the family altar, Steele would have been able to spend enough time to make certain that there would be ample provisions in his supply wagons; as it was, he had to put his men on half-rations only a day after they had marched out of Little Rock and the threat of starvation would be an important reason he failed to reach Shreveport.

In December 1863, when the Lincoln presented his Proclamation of Amnesty and Reconstruction, Radicals and conservatives alike found it highly satisfactory. But defeats in Louisiana and Arkansas aborted the experiment, and by the summer of 1864 Ben Wade and Henry Winter Davis were pushing punitive measures in Congress that Lincoln opposed.[3] Disputes over restoration widened the gulf between Wade and Lincoln; only a few days before the President was shot, Bluff Ben declared: "By God, the sooner he is assassinated, the better."[4] And with Lincoln gone, Radicals decreed a kind of reconstruction that the descendants of Confederates would still be deploring more than a hundred and thirty years later.

Such was the length of the shadow the failure of the federal Red River Expedition cast, making Abraham Lincoln perhaps the most prominent casualty of the fiasco.

<hr/>

"From whom did you receive your orders?" Ben Wade asked General

Banks on December 14, 1864, the first day of the inquiry made by the Joint Congressional Committee on the Conduct of the War into the disaster known as the Red River Expedition. From General Halleck, the former commander of the Union's Department of the Gulf replied. That may have been the answer the committee's chairman expected but it was not the one he wanted. Wade, long the leader of the Radical Republican faction in Congress, was using the investigation of Banks' defeat as a means of sullying the reputation and eroding the power of the real target of the probe: Abraham Lincoln.[5]

Chief inquisitor Wade having urged Banks to "give the committee, in your own language and in your own way, a narrative of what is known as the Red River expedition or campaign," Banks took Bluff Ben at his word and shifted his listeners' attention away from who may have been responsible for the fiasco to a nigh-irrelevant description of the Port Hudson operation in the summer of 1863.[6]

Henry Wager Halleck's name would appear in the record frequently thereafter, but the committee did not require his appearance until February 16, 1865, and then Wade asked only four questions. Old Brains adroitly blocked others by replying to one with these words: "The correspondence, copies of which I have already furnished to the committee, gives all the information of an official character which I have in relation to that expedition."[7]

Wade may have refrained from trying to include Halleck in his list of the blameworthy because the general-in-chief of the Union armies had already lost virtually all of the reputation he had to lose; indeed, with Ulysses Grant's promotion to lieutenant general making its way through Congress, he was facing demotion. During the decades of the "Great Remembering" and subsequently, almost all historians would agree that Halleck had been a disaster. One who had studied the Red River Expedition more carefully than most applied the lash to Halleck in passages such as these:

[It was] *a standard tactic of Halleck in his role as general-in-chief to urge, suggest, persuade, but to avoid whenever possible the responsibility of giving a direct order; and then, if his advice was neglected, to censure as if a command had been disobeyed.*[8]

And:

Banks' reasonable request for specific orders evoked from Halleck a typically nebulous and irritable rejoinder . . . [Halleck] would only state his views and leave Banks free to "adopt such lines and plans for the [Red

River] *campaign" as he might think best. It seems quite evident that this was all Halleck's idea—to transfer to a subordinate all responsibility for decisions and for any possible reverses that might occur . . . In addition, the suspicion arises that perhaps he sensed some possible disaster awaiting Banks in the pine forests of Louisiana.*[9]

Such run-on condemnations did not give effect to what may be termed the Halleck Doctrine. "I hold that a General in command of an army in the field is the best judge of existing conditions," he declared to his commander-in-chief on the night before Major General Ambrose Burnside attacked the Confederate Army of Northern Virginia at Fredericksburg. If—from faraway Washington—Lincoln wanted to issue orders canceling the operation, Halleck told the President, "you must issue them yourself."[10]

Strict adherence to principle was extremely rare in Washington. General Halleck's stubbornness in applying his doctrine contributed to his being called the most unpopular man in the Union capital.[11]

As noted above, Nathaniel Banks did not have enough familiarity with the ways of those in high military command to reach a meeting of the minds with the general-in-chief.[12] And historians who charged Old Brains with hanging the Bobbin Boy out to dry missed the fact that the Halleck Doctrine assumes that "the General in command of an army in the field" is *competent.*

Fredericksburg's casualty list containing more than 12,600 Northerners' names was evidence that Burnside was not competent, not grounds for arguing that Halleck or even Lincoln ought to have stopped him from attacking. The operative errors were first, giving Burnside command, and then continuing him in it. The remedy was to remove him, which on the eve of that tragic battle Halleck lacked the power and Lincoln the presence of mind or maybe the will to do.

Much the same could be said of Nathaniel Banks.

Even so, a respected historian would much later seek to make Halleck a casualty of the Red River Expedition, going so far as to call readers' attention to "the suspicion . . . that perhaps [Halleck] sensed some possible disaster awaiting Banks in the pine forests of Louisiana." Yet this does raise a valid question: To what extent was General Halleck to blame for the disaster in damp sand?

Consider the evidence available in the paper trail:

- "The President regards the opening of the Mississippi River as the first and most important of all our military and naval operations," the general-in-chief wrote in the order to Banks dated November 9, 1862.

"This river being opened, the question arises how the troops and naval forces there can be employed to the best advantage. Two objects are suggested as worthy of your attention." Those were a drive eastward from Vicksburg to "cut off all connexion by rail between northern Mississippi and Mobile and Atlanta," and "to ascend with a naval and military force the Red River as far as it is navigable, and thus open an outlet for the sugar and cotton of northern Louisiana." General Halleck also suggested that the Red River "would form the best base for our operations in Texas." And Halleck closed with these very clear words:

These instructions are not intended to tie your hands or hamper your operations in the slightest degree. So far away from headquarters, you must necessarily exercise your own judgment and discretion in regard to your movements against the enemy, keeping in view that the opening of the Mississippi river is now the great and primary object of your expedition. . .[13]

At about the date of this order, Lincoln and Secretary of War Edwin Stanton were giving the impression that General Banks would be leading troops from the Northeast in a seaborne invasion of Texas. That may have been the only reason the Red River was even mentioned; the President's then-undisclosed priority was (as Halleck stated) on opening the Mississippi and Banks' actual, though still secret, destination was New Orleans. If the broad discretion given Banks was an attempt to avoid responsibility, which seems doubtful in view of Lincoln's subsequent emphasis on opening the Mississippi, the administration would seem to have been at fault—not General Halleck.

- On August 6, 1863, the general-in-chief carried out the wishes of the president, Secretary of State William H. Seward, and Secretary of War Stanton by telegraphing Banks: "There are important reasons why our flag should be restored in some point of Texas with the least possible delay. Do this by land at Galveston, at Indianola, or at any other point you may deem preferable."[14] Four days later Halleck followed this up in a message explaining that the order had been peremptory because of "European complications." After assuring Banks that the authority conferred on him "is not in the slightest degree changed," Halleck offered the *opinion* that the flag planting in Texas could "best and most safely be effected by a combined military and naval movement up Red River to Alexandria, Natchitoches, or Shreveport, and the military occupation of Northern Texas."

And then General Halleck added a sentence that implies more than it conveys: "This would be merely carrying out the plans *proposed by you* at the beginning of the campaign . . . Nevertheless, your choice is left unrestricted."⁵ [Italics supplied.]¹⁵ Why would Halleck refer to the Red River alternative in this way, and at this early date, if he were trying to force Banks to adopt it?

- In a message dated December 30, 1863, General Banks said in a report to the general-in-chief: "The rivers are not yet deep enough to enable us to advance toward the Red River . . . The country is without supplies of any kind. It is my desire, if possible, to get possession of Galveston."¹⁶ Then, on January 23, 1864, he informed Halleck that he would "most cordially cooperate" with Major General Frederick Steele in Arkansas and Rear Admiral David Dixon Porter "in executing your orders."¹⁷

What *orders*?

- In General Halleck's reply dated February 1, 1864, there was no comment regarding Banks' abrupt loss of desire "to get possession of Galveston" and sudden willingness to undertake what would become the Red River Expedition of 1864. Instead, Halleck's message referred to the study of advantages and disadvantages made by Major D. C. Houston that Banks had sent him on January 23 and offered what might be considered reasons Banks could cite if he felt compelled to change his mind again:

The geographical character of the theater of war west of the Mississippi indicates Shreveport as the most important objective point of the operations of a campaign for troops moving from the Teche [Banks'], the Mississippi [A. J. Smith's, borrowed from Sherman], and the Arkansas [Steele's] Rivers. Of course the strategic advantages of this point may be more than counterbalanced by disadvantages of communication and supplies.

General Steele reports that he cannot advance [from Little Rock] to Shreveport this winter unless certain of finding supplies on the Red River and of having there the co-operation of your forces or those of General Sherman. If the Red River is not navigable (and it will require many months to open any other communication to Shreveport), there seems very little prospect of the requisite co-operation or transport of supplies.

It has therefore been left entirely to your discretion, after fully investigat-

ing the question, to adopt this line or any other . . .[18]

General Halleck offered Banks additional ways out: General Frederick Steele's troops might be sent to operate with Sherman east of the Mississippi, and he might not receive the "expected aid from Sherman."[19]

Even if the evidence shows that General Halleck's share of blame for the expedition's failure was much less than has been alleged, however, it is true that in advocating the use of the Red River as a means of approaching Texas Halleck came about as close as he ever would to violating his own doctrine: "I hold that a General in command of an army in the field is the best judge of conditions."

It was also curious that Halleck did not appoint some officer to overall command. As a West Point graduate and the nation's foremost military theoretician he recognized the necessity for a clear chain of command. Earlier in the war he had all but demanded that—for valid reasons, as well as a reward for Grant's capture of Forts Henry and Donelson—he be given control over the military department east of his, then commanded by Major General Don Carlos Buell, and he had obtained it. Why, then, did Halleck allow near-chaos in command relationships to blight the operation's chances for success?

First, consider Banks' very high rank; this precluded William Tecumseh Sherman, for example, from being put in charge. Next, departmental boundaries would have to have been changed. Finally, Halleck had been in Washington long enough to discern that political considerations protected incompetent generals such as Banks and Beast Butler from relief from command by the President. Later, Banks, under oath, assured the Joint Congressional Committee on the Conduct of the War that "I should have acted under either [Sherman or Steele] with perfect satisfaction."[20] But where in the record are offers by him to do that?

Grant, after becoming general-in-chief, suggested that Halleck go to Louisiana and assume supreme command.[21] But that was in early May, and by then the campaign had been botched beyond salvage, much less redemption.

⊹═══⊹

By the middle of May 1864 most of the survivors of the Red River Campaign were returning to the locations they had occupied in March. Actually, Frederick Steele had led his weary and almost-starved troops back into Little Rock—the point of origin for their pointless march—two weeks earlier, on May 3.[22] In all, the Union's force in Arkansas engaged in the

Shreveport drive had numbered a little more than ten thousand and of these, nearly three thousand had been killed, wounded, or reported missing. Not including sutlers' vehicles, the Confederates had captured or destroyed roughly 635 wagons and 2,500 horses and mules. Against these costs the federal commander had next to nothing to offer in the way of achievements.[23]

However, General Steele's results were not quite that deplorable if viewed in terms of military theory. He had at least caused Edmund Kirby Smith to strip Richard Taylor of enough infantry and artillery to deprive his insubordinate subordinate of the opportunity to do more than annoy and delay Nathaniel Banks and David Dixon Porter during the federals' retreats from Pleasant Hill and Loggy Bayou to Grand Ecore and finally to the exposed rocks in the Red River above Alexandria.

Unfortunately for Frederick Steele's reputation, however, there were indications that Kirby Smith had been predisposed to move against the Arkansas threat well before the Union column had moved very far from Little Rock toward Shreveport. Also, it would be difficult for posterity to understand how an "Old Army" officer of West Point graduate Fred Steele's experience could have neglected to bring along enough food and fodder to prevent his having to place his men on half rations only one day away from their base and to appear almost oblivious to this aspect of the risks he was incurring. It took the humiliating defeats of his foraging forces at first Poison Spring and then Marks' Mills to budge him out of Camden. And had the pious Stonewall Jackson been in Steele's boots, he might well have declared (as Jackson did in witnessing the Yankees' retreat at Port Republic in 1862) "he who does not see the hand of God in this is blind, sir, blind!"[24]

Short of Providential intervention, it was passing strange that General Steele gave so little effect to the absence of adequate food and fodder in the country southwest of Little Rock. He had been over the route at least as far as Arkadelphia in 1863. Scouts and couriers could have made fresh checks of conditions in late February or early March of 1864, while Steele was detained at Little Rock carrying out the political duties President Lincoln had assigned him. The hunger of his men and animals certainly had as much to do with Steele's defeat as Edmund Kirby Smith.

True, Steele had made it clear that he did not believe the military plan advocated by Halleck would work and that he wanted no part in its execution. It took a peremptory order from General-in-Chief Grant to squelch his protests. Obedience is the first duty of a soldier and Steele obeyed.

But from battle, murder, and sudden death, the Good Lord or some force had delivered Steele and his survivors. And later, after the finger-pointing began, there would be so many other attractive targets in sight that the sacrifices made by the men in the defeated Arkansas prong of the two federal drives would soon be forgotten.

+=—=+

General Steele was among the officers on both sides who were no more fortunate after the Red River Expedition than they were during it. He commanded a division in the capture of Mobile in 1865, a regiment as a colonel in the postwar army, and died in 1868 of apoplexy resulting from an accident while driving a carriage.[25]

Joseph Bailey, justifiably praised by Rear Admiral David Dixon Porter and General Banks for building the wing dams at Alexandria that saved the Union's gunboats and then creating a bridge out of transports and purloined lumber that enabled Banks' troops and wagons to escape further mauling from Dick Taylor's men, received two brevet promotions—the second, to major general—and the Thanks of the Congress. Few men emerged from the war with such well-deserved recognition. But any satisfaction he may have taken with him into civilian life ended only two years later when Sheriff Bailey of Vernon County, Missouri, was shot and killed by bushwhackers he had arrested.[26]

Pleasant Hill proved to have been the last battle for William Franklin and scapegoats Albert Lee and Charles P. Stone. A. J. Smith went on to fight at Tupelo and Nashville but turned to gentler pursuits (postmaster, city auditor at St. Louis) in 1869 and lived to be eighty-one, a very advanced age for so rugged a soldier. Franklin and Lee found in business the success that had eluded them in uniform.[27] Stone, first victim of Bluff Ben Wade's Star Chamber, became chief of staff of the Egyptian army and later served as chief engineer for construction of the foundation of the Statue of Liberty—within sight of Fort Lafayette in New York harbor, the prison in which back in 1862 Stone had been held in solitary confinement for 50 of the 189 days he was denied not only his liberty but access to all the rights common thieves enjoy under the Constitution.[28]

With the possible exception of Richard Taylor, no other senior officer who participated in the Red River Expedition had as much to lose, in terms of reputation, as A. J. Smith's admirer, Rear Admiral David Dixon Porter. In late March and early April of 1861 then-Lieutenant Porter had aided and abetted Secretary of State William H. Seward in a scheme that had the effect of denying the firepower of the USS *Powhatan* to the naval task force Lincoln sent to resupply Fort Sumter; to the extent Seward's duplicity made Sumter's surrender inevitable, his accomplice Porter might be deemed an accessory to the blunders that made civil war a tragic fact. But as commander of the navy's Mississippi Squadron of gunboats, Porter gave superb support to Grant and Sherman during their many failed attempts to get to within striking distance of Vicksburg in 1863; his running of the fortress city's batteries in April gave Grant the opportunity he had been seeking to launch the campaign that succeeded.

In the process of supporting Grant and Sherman, both as professional as he was, Porter seemed to have gained so much confidence in the ability of his gunboats to support the army's operations, especially in nigh-impossible missions, that he may well have reached somewhat beyond his grasp when he told the managers of the Union's war effort he could take the "Pook turtles" and other vessels required "wherever the sand is damp."[29]

Even so, Porter did just that. His major mistake in the campaign involved the ponderous, underpowered *Eastport*. Damp sand was the prevailing condition in which he operated from Alexandria to Loggy Bayou and back again. His vessels absorbed frightful damage on the way down the Red River but except for the *Eastport*, they survived to serve in other waters.

Of concern to Bluff Ben Wade and his associates on the Joint Congressional Committee on the Conduct of the War, however, was not Porter's success but the influence his boasting regarding his gunboats' capabilities may have had on the thinking of Major General Banks and especially on Banks' decision to go forward with the expedition given the very low level of the Red River at Alexandria in March.

In the course of his testimony on December 14, 1864, Banks approached that subject:

> An officer entrusted with important commands ought to be able to say what can be done in his own profession, and should be willing to take that responsibility. It was hazardous to undertake naval operations upon Red river in that condition of things, two or three hundred miles into the interior, unless there was enough water to float the boats. But it was not for me to decide. That belonged to the naval officers to say.

> Question: Was there obtained information of their ability to navigate the river at that time?
> Answer: It was talked over every thirty minutes in the day. It was conceded by everybody that it was impossible to navigate the river in the condition it was then in. But Admiral Porter thought the river would rise; and he used this expression until our officers were indisposed to talk about it: He said, "that wherever the sand was damp he could run his boats."

"[Porter] had a perfect right to run that risk," Banks conceded, "and accept the responsibility. But he did not do that; he left it apparently to someone else to say that the expedition might not be continued."[30]

On March 7, 1865, Admiral Porter was interrogated by Daniel Gooch:

Question: *Did you hold any conference with General Banks at Alexandria, in relation to the ascent of the river by boats?*

Answer: *I did, and opposed it all I could, until he told me that he should move, and that the success of the operation would depend upon the co-operation of the navy; and then I said I would go if I should lose all my boats.*

Question: *Why did you oppose it?*

Answer: *Because I knew we could not get out again, except by some such miracle as enabled us to get out at last, by hard work and the brains of an eastern man,*

Question: *Did you insist, at any conference with General Banks or his staff, that there was no trouble in making the ascent—that your boats could go anywhere where it was a little damp?*

Answer: *I said that a half-dozen times in joke, for we had gone into a great many queer places. I objected to going up the Red River then, and told them that if they went up they must expect a reverse, so far as losing the boats was concerned.*

Question: *Were you under the command of General Banks?*

Answer: *Not at all; I was perfectly independent of him.*

Question: *Did it not devolve on you, and you alone, to determine whether the boats should make the ascent?*

Answer: *I could not very well decide not to go. There was a communication from General Halleck stating that the department had notified him that the navy would co-operate with General Banks; and therefore as long as a gunboat could float I should do what I could to help him. There was but one thing to do under those circumstances—to run the risk of losing the boats . . . If I had said that I would not go, then it would have been said that I should have tried it, and I did not want to give them that opportunity.*[31]

Not asked, unfortunately, was: What, precisely, did the gunboats do that helped General Banks? Or, put another way, What difference would it have made to the expedition's outcome if Porter had kept his vessels below the rapids?

During Banks' advance from Alexandria to Grand Ecore, General Taylor had already moved toward Mansfield; the presence of the Union warships on the river, then, could have been dispensed with. From just west of Grand Ecore northward Banks' chosen route of march was well beyond the range of Porter's guns. While the retreats from Pleasant Hill and Loggy Bayou to Grand Ecore were taking place the navy was not in positions from which it could provide protection or support to Banks' troops. This was true also of the federals' retreats from Grand Ecore to Alexandria, where the gunboats' plight presented Banks with enormous problems.

But if there was less than met the eye to the navy's role in the operation, Admiral Porter did his cause a real service by providing Secretary of the Navy Welles and Cump Sherman with the reports that had a higher probability of being true than anything sent to Washington by the general commanding. Moreover, Porter wrote with style reflecting a wholly admirable enthusiasm for going beyond duty and giving his best response to every challenge. True, at times he exaggerated the strengths of Confederates he and his men fought and the losses inflicted on the rebels. But this could be considered merely a warm-up for his postwar emergence as a writer of fiction.

David Dixon Porter's naval career advanced steadily from the escape from Alexandria to his retirement. Indeed, he may have been the only senior Union officer to have emerged from the fiasco in damp sand with so few scars.

⊹══⊹

It was curious that Nathaniel Banks would be assigned so much of the blame for the fiasco the Red River Campaign of 1864 turned out to be, when in fact his Confederate opposite number all but assured the federals' escape—yet hardly any voices in the South called for the sacking of Edmund Kirby Smith. In part this reflected Richmond's understandable anxiety over how soon the powerful Army of the Potomac, George Meade's on paper but Ulysses Grant's in fact, would smash Robert E. Lee's vastly outnumbered troops and appear before the city's gates. But the Trans-Mississippi had always been considered a backwater of the war, when anyone east of the Big Muddy gave any thought to it at all.

President Jefferson Davis was only one of a number of officials in his government who seemed interested in Kirby Smith-dom (as some called the Trans-Mississippi) only because of its location. Closing of Southern ports to blockade runners had made the Confederates depend to an increasing extent on such resources as they could still draw from European ships off-loading at ports on Mexico's Gulf coast. From there, wagon trains destined for places east of the Mississippi had to rely on Texas' huge land bridge and roads through Louisiana north of Alexandria to reach rafts which might or might not be lucky enough to get across the broad river during gaps between the Union navy's patrols.

Had it not been for the Mexican ports, Davis might well have written-off Louisiana, Arkansas, and Texas and ordered Kirby Smith to bring such forces as he still had eastward to reinforce Robert E. Lee or Joseph E. Johnston. By early 1864 almost everything that the region could add to the Southern war effort had been extracted from it. Indeed, encouraging words and pious hopes (and not very much of either) were about all that Richmond could afford to send westward.

As has always been the wont of commanders sent to duties far from the seats of government, General Kirby Smith devoted uncounted thousands of words to Davis, Secretary of War Seddon, governors of states in his zone of responsibility, members of the Confederate Congress and of state legislatures, and mayors to complaints of gross neglect and appeals for aid of any sort or description.[32] And when he wrote, the department commander knew or soon learned that his requests would be turned down, the bottom of nearly every jurisdiction's barrel long since having been reached.

Indeed, Edmund Kirby Smith was nigh-devoid of clout in dealing with civilian officials. It was as though the more distant from Shreveport they were, the easier it was for them to ignore this Floridian who had done nothing so far to earn their respect. To some extent this was unfair; Dick Taylor, with no political weight to carry, was a fighter whose audacity made Kirby Smith's enforced dedication to administration and inter-as well as intra-government accord seem all the more timid; and, short of relieving and banishing the widely admired Taylor, there was not much Kirby Smith could do about it.

In all probability Edmund Kirby Smith would have been considerably more effective, and also more successful, had he heeded what used to be termed the *call* to become an Episcopal minister. In his dealings with governors he made every effort to please, to achieve a meeting of the minds acceptable to all concerned, which might have been expected of a conscientious rector in a vast parish plagued with complex problems. But given the circumstances prevailing, the compromises Kirby Smith negotiated proved to be beyond the capabilities of the parties involved to implement.

Put differently, those qualities which might have made the Trans-Mississippi Department's commander an eminent shepherd of a worshipful flock were not particularly helpful to him as the leader of men engaged in the form of insanity called fighting a war to the death for the freedom to be left alone by coercive governments based too far away for the inept politicians directing them to be horsewhipped. Edmund Kirby Smith was totally committed to the Southern cause and was among its most faithful servants. But he was not a killer, and this may well have been what an ancient Greek playwright might have recognized as his tragic flaw.

Yet Kirby Smith won; why dwell on his inadequacies, why set him down as anything less than a successful commander? Because decisions made by what Dick Taylor called Hydrocephalus at Shreveport appear to have prevented the utter destruction of Banks' army and Porter's gunboat flotilla. But did they?

The problem, here, was not so much that Kirby Smith and Taylor never achieved a meeting of the minds regarding strategy, but that the general commanding seemed unable to adopt one and carry it out. At times it was as though this general was not really commanding but thinking out loud, or seeking agreement, while at others he displayed a counterproductive stubbornness in pursuing courses of action from which he would have been wise to abstain.

From his central position at Shreveport, Kirby Smith had the capability of massing his forces, keeping them together, and destroying first one Union column and then the next. This was what Taylor urged him to do, advocating Banks' expedition as the first Union force to be attacked because it was nearer, larger, clearly the greater threat. With Banks out of the picture, the Confederates would then turn and whip Frederick Steele.

Simple and classical though this strategy was, however, Kirby Smith appeared to be more afraid of Steele than of Banks. Curiously, in a message to Taylor dated April 22, Kirby Smith felt compelled to justify the effort he was making in Arkansas:

> *Steele cannot be left in his present position* [near Camden], *strengthened by re-enforcements and supplies, without endangering the fruit of your victories below. He must be driven to fight or to retreat toward the Arkansas* [River] . . . *Retreat is as disastrous to him as defeat.*[33]

Yet Kirby Smith had known before he left Shreveport that Steele was in enough trouble to have veered off toward Camden, and Marmaduke's cavalry had captured the federals' foraging party's wagons at Poison Spring four days before he wrote Taylor. Steele had already been reinforced but this merely aggravated his food shortage.

By contrast, up in Virginia's Wilderness U. S. Grant would snap at an aide who feared Lee's audacity, saying in effect, *Instead of worrying about what the enemy will do to you, think about what you can do to him.*[34]

157

At a minimum Edmund Kirby Smith failed to make either Taylor's or Sterling Price's forces strong enough to defeat Banks or Steele. Taylor routed Banks at Sabine Crossroads by drawing Banks onto a battleground on which the Confederates outnumbered elements of Banks' army; hunger turned Steele back toward Little Rock. And even when the flooded Saline River stalled Steele's retreating troops long enough for Kirby Smith to catch up at Jenkins' Ferry, the Trans-Mississippi Department's commander seriously botched a battle he need not have fought.

Perhaps Kirby Smith simply could not grasp the truth that Sherman put so bluntly—"War is cruelty, and you cannot refine it"—and was unable to focus his mind to produce decisive results. Foggy thinking is reflected in instructions of a sort he gave Taylor in a message dated May 12, at about the time General Banks was preparing to leave Alexandria:

I have every confidence in your ability and judgment, and while I do not wish to restrain you in operations which are extraordinary in results and highly creditable to yourself and command, you cannot exercise too much caution in risking a general engagement or in too far committing your whole force to a position on the river below Alexandria beyond the power of retreat in the event of a disaster.[35]

Consider the opposite, General-in-Chief Henry Halleck's reply to Meade's complaint that he could not locate Lee's army: "If you pursue him and fight him, I think you will find out where he is. I know of no other way."[36]

In Kirby Smith's message to Taylor dated April 22, roughly a week before Jenkins' Ferry, he provided another justification for having reduced Taylor's troop strength in order to chase starving Yankees in central Arkansas:

Ultimate and substantial results, with a field for important military operations, is opened by the capture or dispersion of Steele's force. In both a political and military point of view everything is to be gained for the [Trans-Mississippi] department by its accomplishment. If you are convinced that Banks is retreating to New Orleans, and you can leave Polignac or Wharton in command, I would suggest that you repair here in person. I can place you on duty with your increased rank, and would feel I had left the conduct of operations in safe hands.[37]

On May 24 Dick Taylor replied to this suggestion that if Steele could be whipped something else might be in the offing. "The condition of my

health," he wrote, "precludes the hope that I will be able to participate in a
Missouri campaign." That said, he provided Kirby Smith with a lengthy,
well thought-out plan for the venture. He also condemned the inefficiency
of Hydrocephalus at Shreveport and closed by saying: "I have the honor to
repeat my request previously made, that I may speedily be relieved from
duty in this department."[38]

Four days later, still ill, Taylor wrote another message to his general
commanding—one in which he again referred to the folly of going after
Steele and Kirby Smith's hints regarding a Missouri campaign:

> I cannot conceive what "political and military points of view" are to be ob-
> tained for the Confederacy by abandoning the certain destruction of an
> army of 30,000 men, backed by a huge fleet, to chase after a force of
> 10,000 in full retreat with over 100 miles the start. To accomplish this, to
> me, inscrutable purpose, I was prevented from following up my victories,
> allured to Shreveport by compliments on my readiness to serve under Gen-
> eral Price, and there unexpectedly deprived of the bulk of my army . . .
>
> Your communication closes by inviting me to Arkansas, where "I can
> place you on duty with increased rank, and would feel that I had left the
> conduct of operations in safe hands." What has occurred since you re-
> moved the conduct of operations from my hands after Pleasant Hill to
> change your opinion of my capacity? General, had you then left the con-
> duct of operations in my hands Banks' army would have been destroyed be-
> fore this; the fleet would have been in our hands or blown up by the enemy.
> The moral effect at the North and the shock to public credit would have se-
> riously affected the war . . .
>
> You speak of placing me on duty with increased rank. Has the President
> been pleased to promote me? If so, I have received no notice of it . . . Until
> that time comes I am content, for I have learned from my ancestors that it
> is the duty of a soldier so to conduct himself as to dignify titles and not de-
> rive importance from them . . .
>
> The events of the past few weeks have so filled me with discouragement
> that I much fear I cannot do my whole duty under your command, and I
> ask that you take steps to relieve me as soon as it can be done without injury
> to the service.[39]

"Respectfully returned to General Taylor," Kirby Smith wrote in his En-
dorsement. "This communication is not only improper but unjust. I cannot
believe but that it was written in a moment of irritation or sickness."[40] He
had called Taylor's message of April 24 "objectionable and improper," adding: "The fruits of your victory at Mansfield were secured" by the pursuit of

the Yankees from Camden. "The complete success of the campaign was determined by the overthrow of Steele at Jenkins' Ferry."[41]

What overthrow of Steele? Dick Taylor was justified in wondering. But it was possible that some of Kirby Smith's messages were written by medical director Sol A. Smith, who was said to have hated Taylor. A headquarters hack, rather than a commanding general, seems to likely to have been the author of the reply to Taylor's May 24 comments regarding the inefficiencies of Hydrocephalus at Shreveport. An extract:

> *Seventh:* [Quoting from Taylor's message] *"Meanwhile the troops in the field are without pay, insufficiently supplied with food," &c. As soon as funds were received from Richmond I directed the payment of the army. The chief of the pay department (Major Carr) stated that the troops in the field did not desire a payment before the issue of the new currency; that he had arranged with then perfectly to their satisfaction to await payment until the new currency was received. Major Thomas, chief commissary, states that there is, and was on May 25, abundant supplies at the command of your commissary for the whole army in Louisiana, I inclose [sic] their statements.*[42]

However, there could be no doubt regarding who sent Kirby Smith this message on June 5:

> *You are mistaken in supposing that my communications were intended as complaints. I have no complaints to make. My communications were statements of facts, necessary, in my judgment, to the proper understanding of the campaign. I have not read the story of Gil Blas and the Archbishop to so little purpose as not to know that truth is often considered "objectionable by superiors," but I have not drawn the moral that it is therefore "improper in subordinates to state it."*

General Taylor then gave his interpretation of events, including (among many others) this refutation of Kirby Smith's claims regarding Jenkins' Ferry:

> *At Jenkins' Ferry you attacked with your infantry alone. Nearly 8,000 men were not used at all, either in the fight or after it. This surplus of troops might well have enabled you to leave Walker with me. At Jenkins' Ferry you lost more heavily in killed and wounded than the enemy. This appears from the official report of Steele, confirmed by our officers who were present. You lost two pieces of artillery, which the enemy did not carry off*

because he had previously been deprived of means of transportation by Maxey and Fagan. He burned his pontoon [bridge] for the same reason, and because after crossing the Saline he had no further use for it. He marched to Little Rock after the fight entirely unmolested. He would un-questionably have gone there had the fight never occurred. We do not to-day hold one foot more of Arkansas than if Jenkins' Ferry had never been, and we have a jaded army and 1,000 less soldiers. How, then, was the "complete success of the campaign determined by Steele's overthrow at Jenkins' Ferry?" In truth, the campaign as a whole has been a hideous fail-ure. The fruits of Mansfield have been turned to dust and ashes. Louisiana, from Natchitoches to the Gulf, is a howling wilderness and her people are starving. Arkansas is probably as great a sufferer.

And he closed with a by-then predictable request:

The same regard for duty which led me to throw myself between you and popular indignation and quietly take the blame of your errors compels me to tell you the truth, however objectionable to you. The grave errors you have committed in the recent campaign may be repeated if the unhappy conse-quences are not kept before you. After the desire to serve my country, I have none more ardent than to be relieved from longer serving under your command.[43]

General Edmund Kirby Smith's response was to grant his insubordinate subordinate's most ardent wish, subject to the pleasure of the President. "I would have arrested General Taylor on receipt of his first letter," he wrote Jefferson Davis on June 11, "but acknowledging his merits as a soldier and feeling kindly disposed toward him, I passed it by. I have since borne and forborne with him with a self-control that has been sustained only by love of country and a desire for promoting her best interests." He enclosed three of Taylor's letters. "They are untrue throughout," the general commanding asserted, "and will generally be proved to be so by the simple narrative of events which I have forwarded Your Excellency." A few lines above that statement he had said, "one of us should be relieved." Kirby Smith returned to that point in closing: "I will willingly, with no feeling of envy or abate-ment of interest in the service of my country, turn over my arduous duties and responsibilities to a successor."[44]

Jefferson Davis left Kirby Smith in command, but he refused to allow

Sol Smith (who was a civilian) to replace Brigadier General William R. Boggs as chief of staff. The commander-in-chief approved Dick Taylor's promotion to lieutenant general and ordered him to bring such forces as he could east of the Mississippi, but federal patrolling on the river was so effective that only Taylor got across. In the fall of 1864 he took command of the Department of East Louisiana, Mississippi, and Alabama. Both Taylor and Kirby Smith were among the last to surrender. Kirby Smith later became an educator and the father of ten children. Taylor, highly regarded by many Northern leaders in the postwar period, used his influence to ameliorate reconstruction's harshness. He was also instrumental in obtaining Jefferson Davis' release from solitary confinement at Fort Monroe.

Edmund Kirby Smith would be remembered as an amiable, well-intentioned officer whose services lacked distinction. He was uncommonly fortunate in having Richard Taylor under his command. And Taylor, in turn, owed much of his success to his mentor, General Stonewall Jackson.

Some of Dick Taylor's debts to Jackson were evident in the Louisianan's strategic withdrawal from Alexandria to Mansfield and his setting the trap at Sabine Crossroads that wrecked enough of the federal invasion force to cause its commander to change the expedition's objective from the seizure of Shreveport first to sheer survival and then to holding New Orleans. But other traces of Old Jack's influence were to be found in his ability to motivate men who were nearly always outnumbered, poorly equipped, underpaid if not unpaid—yet who gave Dick Taylor all that he asked of them, and often much more. And like Jackson, Taylor never hesitated to risk his career in order to resist nonsense.

Nathaniel P. Banks, by contrast, never really risked his career. At critical points in the campaign he commanded by consensus, misguided by the notion that he had more to fear from his friends than from the Confederates' bayonets. In the process, he heeded his motto "Success is a Duty" by following another, Save the Surface and You Save All. And as one result, General Banks was not only relieved of his command but summoned to Washington to enlighten the Radical-dominated and prosecutorial-minded Joint Congressional Committee on the Conduct of the War.

Banks was a "political" general, but so was the man who had whipped him. Abraham Lincoln may have overloaded him by adding the duty of preparing Louisiana for restoration to the Union to his military responsibilities, but unlike Dick Taylor, Banks did not protest, much less offer his bare neck to Washington's guillotine. Certainly, Lincoln did his friend no service by allowing him to remain in command of combat troops after his dismal performance in the Shenandoah Valley Campaign of 1862. The amateur acting-general-in-chief saved himself from greater failures by bringing Henry Halleck east to fill that post, in the course of so doing inadvertently making Halleck his mentor. But Banks had no such guide, and Halleck's doctrine precluded him from in effect commanding the expedition from a desk more than a thousand miles away. Worse, Banks' advisors were as inept as he was in coping with the expedition's challenges. Such was the consequence of using a theater of war as a dumping ground for senior officers deemed incompetent in earlier assignments.

And so it was that Bluff Ben Wade subjected his fellow abolitionist and former Congressional colleague to the Star Chamber, even though Banks' defeat was hardly more than an embarrassment at a time when the Union's conquest of the Confederacy seemed imminent. But Abraham Lincoln had been involved in the fiasco from first to last, and any chance to expose the president's lapses and deficiencies was to Wade and his associates as blood in the water is to sharks.

In the controversial committee's majority report issued after months of interrogating witnesses, Chairman Wade indeed scattered blame for the disaster all the way up to the president, whose policies regarding restoration of states such as Louisiana the Radical Republican senator from Ohio bitterly opposed. Bluff Ben was less successful in linking Lincoln and the activities of cotton speculators. Addressing Congress, Wade wrote:

> *Your committee would state that while the object had in view by General Halleck, in urging this expedition, was a military one, with the expectation perhaps of accomplishing some important political result by the occupation of some point in Texas, the general commanding the expedition appears to have had in view the two objects of carrying out measures for the establishment of a State government in Louisiana, and of affording an egress for cotton and other products of that region of the country. And many of the witnesses express the opinion, in which the committee concur, that the attention directed to the accomplishment of these objects exerted a most unfavorable influence upon the expedition.*
>
> *This expedition presents many remarkable features. It was undertaken without the direction of any one, so far as the evidence shows. The authorities at Washington did not furnish the troops which the general commanding considered necessary for the purpose . . . The only orders emanating from Washington . . . were those of the President contained in a permit he gave to Casey and Butler "to go up Red River and purchase cotton" in which he directed the "officers of the army and navy to furnish such assistance as might be desirable."*
>
> *In the absence of all orders requiring this expedition to be undertaken, and after the refusal of the authorities at Washington to furnish the troops*

asked for, it was entered upon by the commanding general, as shown by the evidence; against his judgment and in the belief that it must necessarily fail; and it was prosecuted at immense sacrifice of property, of life, and of valuable time, after the development of facts that utterly precluded all hopes of success. It did not seek to accomplish any distinctly avowed military object, and as a military movement it seems to have been conducted without capacity or discipline. Its only results, in addition to the disgraceful military disasters that attended it, were of a commercial and political character . . .

The political transactions were shown by the holding of elections in the camps of the army while engaged in the expedition, with the view of reorganizing civil government in Louisiana. The attempt to do this was clearly a usurpation on the part of the military authorities, the execution of which was as weak and inefficient as the attempt was improper and illegal.[45]

Congressman Daniel Gooch's minority report was more sympathetic toward General Banks, implying that he may have been intimidated by Halleck.[46] But the whipping Banks took at Sabine Crossroads, wrote Gooch, "was not of sufficient importance to cause the failure of this expedition."[47] He was on somewhat firmer ground in a later passage: "The extent of the disaster . . . was very greatly exaggerated at the time."[48] As to cotton, Gooch held that seizures caused no delays in military operations. As to the elections Wade had called "improper and illegal," Gooch rather lamely pointed out that it did not appear that they "influenced or controlled the expedition to the slightest degree."[49]

Perhaps, but Bluff Ben and Gooch both missed the central fact about the fiasco: the Red River was pro-Confederate.

Senator Benjamin Franklin Wade and his Radical cohorts, even then on their way to commit the atrocity known later as reconstruction, all but dropped Banks. As had been his wont regarding the Committee on the Conduct of the War, Lincoln had kept his distance from the proceedings. Banks, who had been in Washington most of the time since General Canby replaced him in all but nominal functions at New Orleans, pressed the president to restore him to military command. This, Lincoln adamantly refused to do; instead, he kept him at the capital acting as a lobbyist, using his old connections to advance the restoration plan in Congress. Banks was on his way back to New Orleans to work on local political problems in April 1865 when Lincoln was assassinated.[50]

For a time after the war ended, Banks considered settling in New Orleans and practicing law. But late in 1865 he returned to Massachusetts and his first love, politics. Soon he was back in Washington as a member of the House of Representatives. "Banks chases office in every latitude," said

Congressman Daniel H. Gooch

one of his critics. "He will pursue it by rail, on horseback, by still-hunting—or he will take it on the wing."[51]

Back in the old familiar Congressional milieu of go along to get along, the former witness before the Joint Committee on the Conduct of the War allowed himself to be nudged into joining the Radicals. Banks, declared Gideon Welles, had "neither the courage nor the ability to try anything else."[52] He served in ten Congresses, although not continuously, before he retired in 1890. Four years later, the Bobbin Boy died at his home in Waltham.[53]

+====+

Dick Taylor's Louisianans and Texans discouraged the Yankees from attempting further molestation during the rest of 1864 and the early months of 1865. But the people in the Trans-Mississippi states suffered greatly during the decades in which Radical-driven reconstruction policies prevailed. Short of independence, even in defeat, the people in Texas, Louisiana, and Arkansas would have been far better off had Abraham Lincoln's relatively mild restoration provisions not been casualties of the Red River Expedition. As it was, it would take a hundred years for the region to recover, and in some respects it may never.

As was the case with better-known battles—Shiloh, Fredericksburg, Stones River, Chancellorsville—the Red River Campaign settled nothing, at enormous cost. Sherman's "bummers," reflecting human imperfection writ very large, may have displayed more nigh-savage cruelty in their mindless devastation of portions of Georgia and the Carolinas. But the damage done by the Yankees in the Red River Valley of Louisiana was shocking enough for General Taylor to write on April 24, 1864:

> The destruction of this country by the enemy exceeds anything in history. For many miles every dwelling-house, every Negro cabin, every cotton-gin, every corn-crib, and even chicken houses have been burned to the ground, every fence torn down and the fields torn up by the hoofs of horses and the wheels of wagons. Many hundreds of persons are utterly without shelter.[54]

Even so, the challenges presented during the campaign provoked a host of responses marked by the courage and honor and hope and pride and compassion and pity and sacrifice and endurance that men on both sides conveyed, values that would motivate generations yet unborn not only to survive the adversities they would face, but to prevail over them.

166

NOTES

CHAPTER 1

1. U.S. Congress, Report of the Joint Committee on the Conduct of the War (CCW), *Red River Expedition*, 3.

2. T. Harry Williams, *Lincoln and the Radicals*, 9–12.

3. This engagement is covered in detail by Byron Farwell in *Ball's Bluff and its Long Shadow*, and by Kim Bernard Holien in *Battle at Ball's Bluff*.

4. Williams, 55–61.

5. *Ibid*, 64.

6. *Ibid*, 66–67.

7. Fred Harvey Harrington, *Fighting Politician: Major General N. P. Banks*, 62; Patricia L. Faust, editor, *Historical Times Encyclopedia of the Civil War*, 38.

8. General Banks' military ineptitude has been documented by most historians of Jackson's Shenandoah Valley Campaign and General Robert E. Lee's victory at Second Manassas (Bull Run). Harrington, Banks' biographer, was candid on this point.

9. CCW, iii–iv.

10. Ludwell H. Johnson, *Red River Campaign: Politics and Cotton in the Civil War*, 6.

11. *Ibid.*, 8.

12. *Ibid.*, 6.

13. Rupert Norval Richardson, Ernest Wallace, and Adrian N. Anderson, *Texas: The Lone Star State*, 222–227.

14. Johnson, 7–8.

15. Faust, 98–99.

16. Johnson, 10–11.

17. *Ibid.*, 11.

18. *Ibid.*, 12–13.

19. E. P. Long with Barbara Long, *The Civil War Day–by–Day*, 204.

20. Faust, 98–99.

21. David Herbert Donald, *Lincoln*, 330.

22. *Ibid.*, 341, 348–349.

23. Frances H. Kennedy, editor, *The Civil War Battlefield Guide*, Herman Hattaway, "The Seven Days Campaign," 58; Robert K. Krick, "Cedar Mountain," 70; John Hennessy, "Second Manassas," 74.

24. Johnson, 18.

25. *Ibid.*, 14–17.

26. All Civil War casualty figures are suspect. The components of this one are the Shenandoah Valley Campaign, 7,000; The Seven Days, 15,849; Cedar Mountain, 2,500; Second Manassas, 9,931; Various, 3,895; and Sharpsburg (Antietam), 13,000.

27. Shelby Foote, *The Civil War*, I, 763–764; Johnson, 16, 24; Stephen E. Ambrose, *Halleck: Lincoln's Chief of Staff*, 108–111.

28. Johnson, 24, 21–22.

29. *Ibid.*, 20.

30. *Ibid.*, 21.

31. *Ibid.*, 19; *War of the Rebellion: Official Records of the Union and Confederate Armies*, Series III, Volume II, 691–692.

32. Johnson, 22–23.

33. *Ibid.*, 24–28.

34. *Ibid.*, 28.

35. A. Wilson Greene, "Fredericksburg," in Kennedy, *The Civil War Battlefield Guide*, 97.

36. Herman Hattaway and Archer Jones, *How the North Won*, 293, 300, 309, 312–315; Lloyd Lewis, *Sherman: Fighting Prophet*, 257–259; Ambrose, 112–115.

37. Harrington, 117–119.

38. Richard Taylor, *Destruction and Reconstruction*, 125–146.

39. Faust, 596. For a concise but clear account of the fight for Port Hudson, see Kennedy, editor, *The Civil War Battlefield Guide*, Lawrence Lee Hewitt, "Port Hudson," 146–149.

40. Harrington, 119–120.

41. *Ibid.*, 119; Johnson, 33.

42. Harrington, 119–120.

43. Ulysses S. Grant, *Memoirs and Selected Letters of U. S. Grant*, compiled by Mary Drake and William S. McFeely, 350.

44. Taylor, 158–160.

45. Harrington, 120.

46. *Ibid.*

47. *Ibid.*, 121–122.

48. *Ibid.*, 121.

49. *Ibid.*, 122; Faust, 596–597.

50. Harrington, 122.

51. *Ibid.*, 120; Faust, 596.

52. Harrington, 122. Disease raised Banks' losses to about 10,000.

53. Faust, 596–597.

54. Harrington, 140.

55. *Ibid.*, 125.

56. CCW, 3–4.

57. Taylor, 164–168.

58. Harrington, 128; Johnson, 36, 42.

59. Harrington, 128; Hattaway and Jones, 430–432.

60. *O. R.*, XXVI, Part 1, 661.

61. *Ibid.*, 673.

62. *Ibid.*, 695–697; CCW, 364.

63. Harrington, 128–130.

64. *The New Encyclopedia Britannica*, Volume 24, 44; Henry Bamford Parkes, *A History of Mexico*, 252–258.

65. George H. Gordon, *From Brook Farm to Cedar Mountain*, 191–192.

66. *O. R.*, XXVI, 1, 287–288; Johnson, 37.

67. Johnson, 37; Faust, 650.

68. Harrington, 118.

69. CCW, 365.

70. *Ibid.*, 366–367; O, R., XXVI, 1, 290–292.

71. CCW, 365–366.

72. Harrington, 130–132; CCW, 361–362.

73. Harrington, 131.

74. *Ibid.*, 133.

75. *Ibid.*

76. *Ibid.*, 140–144; Johnson, 45–46; Donald, 467–474.

77. Johnson, 46–47.

78. Herman Haupt, *Reminisences*, 177.

79. Harrington, 142–143.

80. *Ibid.*, 143; Johnson, 46.

81. Johnson, 85.

82. Faust, 715.

CHAPTER 2

1. U.S. Congress, Report of the Joint Committee on the Conduct of the War (CCW), *Red River Expedition*, 5–6.

2. CCW, xvii; *War of the Rebellion: Official Records of the Union and Confederate Armies*, Series I, Volume XV, 590–591.

3. Shelby Foote, *The Civil War*, III, 15–16.

4. CCW, xxv.

5. Ludwell H. Johnson, *Red River Campaign: Politics and Cotton in the Civil War*, 42, 84; Lloyd Lewis, *Sherman: Fighting Prophet*, 342.

6. CCW, xxiv.

7. *Ibid.*, xxv.

8. *Ibid.*, xxii–xxiii.

9. *Ibid.*, xxiii

10. *Ibid.*, xxvi–xxvii; O. R., XXXIV, 2, 133.

11. Johnson, 47, 66; CCW, 355.

12. CCW, xxviii.

13. Johnson, 82.

14. *Ibid.*, 84.

15. *Ibid.*, 82–84.

16. Foote, III, 29.

17. Patricia L. Faust, editor, *Historical Times Encyclopedia of the Civil War*, 895.

18. *Ibid.*

19. Richard Taylor, *Destruction and Reconstruction*, Introduction by Edward C. Bearss, ix–x; Faust, 743–744; Mark M. Boatner, III, *The Civil War Dictionary*, 827–828.

20. Taylor (Bearss), xix, xxvi.

21. Faust, 515; Taylor, 127, 162–163, 191–194.

22. Faust, 321.

23. *Ibid.*, 590; Taylor, 178–179.

24. Faust, 797; Taylor, 172.

25. Faust, 523; Taylor, 162–163, 191–192, 209–211.

26. Faust, 345–346 (Harrison), 438 (Liddell), 470 (Major); Taylor, 148, 184 (Vincent), 185–186 (Buchel and DeBray).

27. Taylor, 164, 177.

28. Johnson, 86.

29. *Ibid.*, 88–89.

30. Taylor, 178, 186.

31. *Ibid.*, 186–187; Johnson, 119–122.

32. Johnson, 122; O. R., XXXIV, 1, 522.

33. CCW, 28.

34. Ibid., 7.

35. Boatner, 303–304; Faust, 285.

36. Johnson, 98.

37. Faust, 428.

38. *Ibid.*, 694; Johnson, 89–91.

39. Johnson, 91–94.

40. *Ibid.*, 94–96, 98; Taylor, 180–183.

41. Johnson, 85, 170; O. R., XXXIV, 1. 616.

42. Johnson, 170–171; O. R., XXXIV, 2. 638–707.

43. Johnson, 171–172.

44. *Ibid.*, 101–103.

45. CCW, 18.

46. Johnson, 102–103.

47. *Ibid.*, 105–106; O. R., XXXIV, 2, 610–611, 494.

48. Johnson, 111; O. R., XXXIV, 1, 179–180.

49. Johnson, 108–109.

50. *Ibid.*, 107–108.

51. *Ibid.*, 120–121; O. R., XXXIV, 1, 515.

52. Johnson, 123.

53. Taylor, 183–184; Johnson, 96–97.

54. Taylor, 184.

55. Johnson, 99–100.

56. *Ibid.*, 110–111.

57. O. R., XXXIV, 2, 179–180.

58. John G. Nicolay and John Hay, *Abraham Lincoln: A History*, VIII, 291.

59. Taylor, 183–185.

CHAPTER 3

1 U.S. Congress, Report of the Joint Committee on the Conduct of the War (CCW), *Red River Expedition*, 281.

2. *Ibid.*, 285.

3. *Ibid.*, 286–287.

4. T. Harry Williams, *Lincoln and the Radicals*, 69.

5. Ludwell H. Johnson, *Red River Campaign: Politics and Cotton in the Civil War*, 117–118.

6. *Ibid.*, 113–116.

7. *Ibid.*, 115; *Official Records of the Union and Confederate Navies in the War of the Rebellion*, Series I, Volume 26, 60.

8. Johnson, 122; Joseph Howard Parks, *General Edmund Kirby Smith, C.S.A.*, 384.

9. Johnson, 122–123.

10. *Ibid.*, 172–173.

11. *Ibid.*, 171–173.

12. *Ibid.*, 176–177.

13. *Ibid.*, 129–131.

14. *Ibid.*, 131.

15. *Ibid.*; *War of the Rebellion: Official Records of the Union and Confederate Armies*, Series I, Volume XXXIV, Part 1, 526.

16. Johnson, 123; O. R., XXXIV, 1, 528.

17. CCW, 57.

18. *Ibid.*, 57–63.

19. *Ibid.*, 58.

20. *Ibid.*, 63–64.

21. *Ibid.*, 58.

22. *Ibid.*, 58–59.

23. *Ibid.*, 59.

24. *Ibid.*

25. *Ibid.*

26. *Ibid.*, 60.

27. *Ibid.*, 29.
28. Johnson, 132.
29. *Ibid.*, 132–133.
30. *Ibid.*, 132.
31. *Ibid.*
32. *Ibid.*
33. CCW, 30.
34. *Ibid.*, 60.
35. *Ibid.*
36. *Ibid.*
37. *Ibid.*, 10.
38. *Ibid.*, 30.
39. Johnson, 132–135; Taylor, 190–191. An excellent but relatively brief account of the battle of Mansfield (in the North, Sabine Crossroads) is to be found in Shelby Foote's *The Civil War*, III, 41–46.
40. CCW, 61.
41. *Ibid.*
42. *Ibid.*, 11.
43. *Ibid.*, 61.
44. Johnson, 134–135.
45. *Ibid.*, 135; Taylor, 191–192.
46. Johnson, 135.
47. Taylor, 192.
48. Johnson, 135.
49. CCW, 38; O. R., XXXIV, 1, 266–267.
50. Johnson, 136.
51. *Ibid.*
52. *Ibid.*
53. *Ibid.*, 137.
54. *Ibid.*, 136–138.
55. *Ibid.*, 142.
56. *Ibid.*, 139.
57. *Ibid.*, 138.
58. *Ibid.*, 138–139.
59. *Ibid.*, 146–147.
60. Taylor, 193.
61. *Ibid.*
62. Johnson, 140–141.
63. Taylor, 193.

CHAPTER 4

1. Ludwell H. Johnson, *Red River Campaign: Politics and Cotton in the Civil War*, 146; U.S. Congress, Report of the Joint Congressional Committee on the Conduct of the War (CCW), *Red River Expedition*, 77.

2 CCW, 77.

3 *Ibid.*, 179.

4 George H. Gordon, *From Brook Farm to Cedar Mountain*, 191–192.

5 Johnson, 146–147.

6 *Ibid.*, 147–148.

7 *Ibid.*, 148–150.

8 *Ibid.*, 150–151.

9 *Ibid.*, 151–152; *War of the Rebellion: Official Records of the Union and Confederate Armies*, Series I, Volume XXXIV, Part 1, 308; Part 3, 99.

10 CCW, 62.

11 *Ibid.*

12 Johnson, 153.

13 Taylor, 183–184.

14 *Ibid.*, 184; Johnson, 153.

15 Johnson, 153.

16 *Ibid.*, 153–154;

17 Taylor, 195.

18 *Ibid.*, 194–195.

19 *Ibid.*,195–196; O. R., XXXIV, 1, 566–567.

20 Johnson, 155.

21 Taylor, 197.

22 Johnson, 156.

23 *Ibid.* 156–157.

24 *Ibid.* 157; Taylor, 199.

25 Johnson, 157–162.

26 *Ibid.* 162.

27 *Ibid.* 162–163.

28 CCW, 35.

29 *Ibid.*

30 Johnson, 163–164.

31 *Ibid.*,168.

32 CCW, 62–63.

33 *Ibid.*,13.

34 Taylor, 200.

35 *Ibid.*,201.

36 Johnson, 180–181.

37 Patricia L. Faust, editor, *Historical Times Encyclopedia of the Civil War*, 52.

38 Johnson, 181.

39 *Ibid.*,117–118, 207–208.

40 *Ibid.*,207–208.

41 *Ibid.*,208.

42 *Ibid.*,209; *Official Records of the Union and Confederate Navies*, Volume 26, 60.

43 Johnson, 209; CCW, 203.

44 Johnson, 177–178.

45 *Ibid.*,176–178.

46 Faust, 695.

47 Taylor, 207.

48 *Ibid.*,207–208.

49 *Ibid.*,208.

50 *Ibid.*

51 *Ibid.*,212–213; Johnson, 181–183; Robert L. Kerby, *Kirby Smith's Confederacy*, 311.

52 Taylor, 208–209.

53 Johnson, 210–211.

54 *Ibid.*,211.

55 O. R. N., 26, 789.

56 *Ibid.*,50.

57 *Ibid.*,54–55.

58 *Ibid.*,49.

59 Taylor, 209.

60 Johnson, 213.

61 *Ibid.*

62 *Ibid.*,213–214.

63 *Ibid.*,214.

CHAPTER 5

1 Ludwell H. Johnson, *Red River Campaign: Politics and Cotton in the Civil War*, 206.

2 U.S. Congress, Report of the Joint Committee on the Conduct of the War (CCW), *Red River Expedition*, 238.

3 *Ibid.*, 239–240.

4 *Official Records of the Union and Confederate Navies in the War of the Rebellion (O. R. N.)*, Series I, Volume 26, 56.

5 *Ibid.*, 64.

6 *Ibid.*, 48.

7 Johnson, 214, 220.

8 CCW, 163.

9 Johnson, 243–244.

10 CCW, 166.

11 *Ibid.*
12 *Ibid.*, 167.
13 *Ibid.*
14 *Ibid.*
15 *Ibid.*, 169.
16 *Ibid.*
17 Johnson, 216.
18 Kim Bernard Holien, *Battle at Ball's Bluff*, 132.
19 Patricia L. Faust, editor, *Historical Times Encyclopedia of the Civil War*, 720.
20 CCW, 190.
21 CCW, 32.
22 Holien, 134–135; Johnson, 218–219.
23 CCW, 17.
24 *Ibid.*, 185–186.
25 *Ibid.*, 186.
26 *Ibid.*, 17.
27 O. R., XXXIV, 1, 610–611; Johnson, 105–106.
28 CCW, 14–15.
29 Johnson, 221.
30 *Ibid.*, 222–223; Taylor, 213–214.
31 Johnson, 221–222.
32 Taylor, 214–216.
33 Shelby Foote, *The Civil War*, II, 921–924; William Tecumseh Sherman, *Memoirs of General W. T. Sherman*, I, 414–424.
34 Sherman, 365.
35 Johnson, 223–225.
36 *Ibid.*, 221–222.
37 *Ibid.*, 222.
38 *Ibid.*, 226.
39 Faust, 817–818.
40 Johnson, 226.
41 *Ibid.*
42 Taylor, 213–214.
43 Johnson, 224.
44 *Ibid.*, 224–255.
45 *Ibid.*, 224.
46 Taylor, 229.
47 Johnson, 222–225.
48 O. R. N., 26, 72.
49 *Ibid.*, 72–73.
50 *Ibid.*, 73.
51 Faust, 234.

52 *O. R. N.*, 26, 73–74.

53 *Ibid.*, 79.

54 *Ibid.*, 74.

55 *Ibid.*

56 David Dixon Porter, *Incidents and Anecdotes*, quoted in H. Allen Gosnell, *Guns on Western Waters*, 254–255.

57 *Ibid.*, 254.

58 *Ibid.*, 255.

59 *O. R. N.*, 26, 167, 169.

60 *Ibid.*, 74.

61 *Ibid.*, 74–75.

62 *Ibid.*, 75.

63 Johnson, 239.

64 *O. R. N.*, 26, 176.

65 *Ibid.*

66 *Ibid.*, 81.

67 *Ibid.*, 82.

68 *Ibid.*, 176.

69 *Ibid.*, 76.

70 *Ibid.*

71 *Ibid.*

72 *Ibid.*, 75.

73 Taylor, 214–216.

74 *Ibid.*, 215.

75 Johnson, 226–228.

76 *Ibid.*, 228–232.

77 *Ibid.*, 232.

78 Taylor, 215–216.

79 *Ibid.*, 216.

CHAPTER 6

1 *Official Records of the Union and Confederate Navies in the War of the Rebellion* (*O. R. N.*), Series I, Volume 26, 93–95.

2 Ludwell H. Johnson, *Red River Campaign: Politics and Cotton in the Civil War*, 243.

3 *War of the Rebellion: Official Records of the Union and Confederate Armies*, Series I, Volume XXXIV, Part 3, 316.

4 *Ibid.*, 316–317; Johnson, 258.

5 Johnson, 176.

6 *Ibid.*, 178–179.

7 *Ibid.*, 179–180.

8 *Ibid.*, 184–185.

9 *Ibid.*, 185–186.
10 *Ibid.*, 186; O. R., XXXIV, 1, 849.
11 Johnson, 187–188.
12 O. R., XXXIV, 1, 661–663.
13 *Ibid.*, Part 3, 162, 267–268; Johnson, 199–189.
14 CCW, 164–166, 172.
15 O. R., XXXIV, 3, 190–192.
16 Johnson, 190–191.
17 *Ibid.*, 189–190.
18 *Ibid.*, 190–193.
19 *Ibid.*, 193–194.
20 O. R., XXXIV, 3, 190–192.
21 Johnson, 194.
22 *Ibid.*
23 Richard Taylor, *Destruction and Reconstruction*, 208–209; CCW, 238.
24 Johnson, 195.
25 O. R., XXXIV, 1, 541–543.
26 *Ibid.*, 543; Joseph Howard Parks, *General Edmund Kirby Smith, C.S.A.*, 405.
27 Johnson, 195.
28 Johnson, 195–196.
29 *Ibid.*, 196.
30 *Ibid.*
31 *Ibid.*, 197; O. R., XXXIV, 1, 677.
32 Johnson, 197.
33 *Ibid.*
34 *Ibid.*, 197–198.
35 *Ibid.*, 197–199.
36 *Ibid.*, 198–199.
37 *Ibid.*, 198–200.
38 *Ibid.*, 200–201.
39 *Ibid.*, 200.
40 *Ibid.*, 201–202.
41 Taylor, 224–225.
42 O. R., XXXIV, 3, 332–333.
43 *Ibid.*, 331–332.
44 Johnson, 246.
45 O. R., XXXIV, 3, 409–410.
46 *Ibid.*, 332–333.
47 Johnson, 250.
48 O. R., XXXIV, 4, 674.
49 *Ibid.*, 1, 542.
50 Parks, 411, 411n.

51 *O. R.*, XXXIV, 1, 476.

CHAPTER 7

1 U.S. Congress, Report of the Joint Committee on the Conduct of the War (CCW), *Red River Expedition*, 169.

2 Patricia L. Faust, editor, *Historical Times Encyclopedia of the Civil War*, 114–115; Henry Walke, in Johnson and Buel, editors, *Battles and Leaders of the Civil War (B&L)*, I, 433–435; Shelby Foote, *The Civil War*, I, 201–204.

3 Foote, I, 312–313.

4 Faust, 115.

5 Ludwell H. Johnson, *Red River Campaign: Politics and Cotton in the Civil War*, 249.

6 *Ibid.*, 249–250.

7 James G. Wilson, quoted in H. Allen Gosnell, *Guns on Western Waters*, 260–261.

8 *Ibid.*, 263.

9 Johnson, 254.

10 *Ibid.*, 254–255; *Official Records of the Union and Confederate Navies in the War of the Rebellion (O. R. N.)*, Series I, Volume 26, 113.

11 Johnson, 257.

12 *Ibid.*

13 *O. R. N.*, 26, 113.

14 *Ibid.*

15 *Ibid.*

16 *Ibid.*, 114.

17 Wilson, in Gosnell, *Guns on Western Waters*, 262.

18 CCW, 82–83.

19 *O. R. N.*, 26, 137.

20 Johnson, 264.

21 *O. R. N.*, 26, 131.

22 *Ibid.*, 136.

23 *Ibid.*

24 *Ibid.*, 131.

25 Johnson, 264.

26 Johnson, 264.

27 *O. R. N.*, 26, 140.

28 *Ibid.*, 140–141.

29 *Ibid.*, 141.

30 *Ibid.*, 131–132.

31 *Ibid.*, 142.

32 *Ibid.*

33 *Ibid.*, 143.

34 *Ibid.*, 144.

35 *Ibid.*, 132.

36 The *Carondelet, Louisville, Mound City, and Pittsburg* were among the seven gunboats called "Pook Turtles" after Samuel M. Pook, their designer. See Faust, 593.

37 O. R. N., 26, 156.

38 *Ibid.*, 132.

39 Johnson, 268–269.

40 *Ibid.*, 270.

41 *Ibid.*, quoting Lawrence Van Alstyne, *Diary of an Enlisted Man*, 320–321.

42 Johnson, 271.

43 *Ibid.*, 268, 270–272.

44 O. R. N., 26, 173.

45 Johnson, 254.

46 Foote, III, 85–86.

47 *War of the Rebellion: Official Records of the Union and Confederate Armies*, Series I, Volume XXXIV, Part 1, 311.

48 Foote, III, 84.

49 O. R., XXXIV, 1, 592.

50 *Ibid.*, 592–593.

51 *Ibid.*, 211.

52 *Ibid.*, 593.

53 Johnson, 273.

54 O. R., XXXIV, 1, 593.

55 *Ibid.*, 594; Foote, III, 86–87.

56 O. R., XXXIV, 1, 212; Foote, III, 87–89.

CHAPTER 8

1 *War of the Rebellion: Official Records of the Union and Confederate Armies*, Series I, Volume XXXIV, Part 1, 594.

2. Unprecedented, that is, for the United States of America.

3. David Herbert Donald, *Lincoln*, 471–474, 509–512.

4. Hans L. Trefousse, *Benjamin Franklin Wade: Radical Republican From Ohio*, 246.

5. *Ibid.*, 240–241.

6. Report of the Joint Congressional Committee on the Conduct of the War (CCW), *Red River Expedition*, 3.

7. *Ibid.*, 227.

8. Ludwell H. Johnson, *Red River Campaign: Politics and Cotton in the Civil War*, 41. It is with deep regret that I must disagree with a scholar to whom all of us who write about this campaign owe debts greater than we can ever repay.

9. *Ibid.*, 82.

10. Herman Haupt, *Reminiscences*, 177.
11. Mark M. Boatner, III, *The Civil War Dictionary*, 367.
12. See page 44, above.
13. O. R., XV, 590–591; CCW, iii–iv.
14. *Ibid.*, XXVI, 1, 672.
15. *Ibid.*, 673.
16. *Ibid.*, 888–889.
17. *Ibid.*, XXXIV, 2, 133.
18. *Ibid.*, 211–212.
19. *Ibid.*, 212.
20. CCW, 6.
21. Johnson, 246.
22. *Ibid.*, 202.
23. *Ibid.*, 203.
24. Robert G. Tanner, *Stonewall in the Valley*, 306.
25. Patricia L. Faust, editor, *The Historical Times Encyclopedia of the Civil War*, 715.
26. *Ibid*, 33.
27. *Ibid.*, 285 (Franklin), 428 (Lee), 694 (Smith), 720 (Stone).
28. General Stone was never told why he was arrested and punished. His treatment by Wade and Stanton, and arguably Lincoln, ranks high among the incidents in which injustice has prevailed.
29. CCW, 8–9, 275.
30. *Ibid.*, 8.
31. *Ibid.*, 275.
32. Joseph Howard Parks, *General Edmund Kirby Smith, CSA*, Chapter XI, 306–344.
33. O. R. XXXIV, 1, 534–535.
34. Shelby Foote, *The Civil War*, III, 172–173.
35. O. R. XXXIV, 1, 537.
36. Kenneth P. Williams, *Lincoln Finds a General*, II, 769.
37. O. R. XXXIV, 1, 534–535.
38. *Ibid.*, 543–545.
39. *Ibid.*, 541–543.
40. *Ibid.*, 543.
41. *Ibid.*, 545–546.
42. *Ibid.*, 538–539.
43. *Ibid.*, 546–548.
44. *Ibid.*, 540–541.
45. CCW, xiv–xv.
46. *Ibid.*, xxxii–xxxiv.
47. *Ibid.*, xl.

48. *Ibid.*, xlv.
49. *Ibid.*, xlix.
50. Fred Harvey Harrington, *Fighting Politician: Major N. P. Banks,* 163–166.
51. *Ibid.*, 169.
52. *Ibid.*, 170.
53. Boatner, 42.
54. O. R. XXXIV, 1, 581.

BIBLIOGRAPHY

Ambrose, Stephen E. *Halleck: Lincoln's Chief of Staff.* Baton Rouge: Louisiana State University Press, 1962.

Basler, Roy P., editor. *The Collected Works of Abraham Lincoln.* 9 vols. New Brunswick: Rutgers University Press, 1953–1955.

Boatner, Mark M. III. *The Civil War Dictionary.* New York: McKay, 1959.

Catton, Bruce. *Grant Takes Command.* Boston: Little, Brown, 1968.

Davis, William C. *Jefferson Davis: The Man and His Hour.* New York: Harper Collins, 1991.

Donald, David Herbert. *Lincoln.* New York: Simon & Schuster, 1995.

Elliott, Charles Winslow. *Winfield Scott: The Soldier and the Man.* New York: Macmillan, 1937.

Encyclopedia Britannica, Inc. *The New Encyclopedia Britannica.* 15th Edition. Chicago: Encyclopedia Britannica, Inc., 1994.

Esposito, Vincent J., chief editor. *The West Point Atlas of American Wars.* 2 vols. New York: Praeger, 1959.

Farwell, Byron. *Ball's Bluff and Its Long Shadow.* McLean, Va.: EPM Publications, 1990.

Faust, Patricia L., editor. *Historical Times Encyclopedia of the Civil War.* New York: Harper & Row, 1986.

Fehrenbacher, Don E., editor. *Abraham Lincoln: Speeches and Writings 1859–1865.* Second of 2 vols. New York: Library of America, 1989.

Foote, Shelby. *The Civil War.* 3 vols. New York: Random House, 1958, 1963, 1974.

Fuller, J. F. C. *The Generalship of Ulysses S. Grant.* New York: Dodd, Mead, 1929.

Gordon, George H. *From Brook Farm to Cedar Mountain.* Boston: Osgood,1883.

Gosnell, H. Allen. *Guns on Western Waters.* Baton Rouge: Louisiana State University Press, 1949.

Grant, Ulysses S. *Ulysses S. Grant: Memoirs and Selected Letters.* Compiled by Mary Drake and William S. McFeely. New York: Library of America, 1990.

Harrington, Fred Harvey. *Fighting Politician: N. P. Banks.* Westport, Conn.: Greenwood Press, 1947.

Haupt, Herman. *Reminiscences.* Milwaukee: Wright & Joy, 1901.

Hoehling, A. A. *Damn the Torpedoes!* Winston-Salem, John F. Blair, 1989.

Holien, Kim Bernard. *Battle at Ball's Bluff.* Orange, Va.: Moss Publications, 1985.

Johnson, Ludwell H. *Red River Campaign: Politics and Cotton in the Civil War*. Baltimore: Johns Hopkins University Press, 1959.

Johnson, Robert U., and C. C. Buel, editors. *Battles and Leaders of the Civil War*. New York: Century, 1887–1888. 4 vols.

Jones, Archer. *Civil War Command & Strategy*. New York: Free Press, 1992.

Josephy, Alvin M. *The Civil War in the American West*. New York: Knopf, 1992.

Kennedy, Frances H., editor. *The Civil War Battlefield Guide*. Boston: Houghton Mifflin, 1990.

Kerby, Robert L. *Kirby Smith's Confederacy*. New York: Columbia University Press, 1972).

Leech, Margaret. *Reveille in Washington*. New York: Harper, 1941.

Lewis, Lloyd. *Sherman: Fighting Prophet*. New York: Harcourt, Brace, 1932.

Livermore, Thomas L. *Numbers and Losses in the Civil War in America, 1861–1865*. Boston: Houghton Mifflin, 1901.

Long, E. B. *The Civil War, Day by Day: An Almanac, 1861–1865*. Garden City: Doubleday, 1971.

McPherson, James M. *Battle Cry of Freedom: The Civil War Era*. New York: Oxford, 1988.

Marszalek, John F. *Sherman: A Soldier's Passion for Order*. New York: Free Press, 1992.

Miers, Earl Schenck. *Lincoln Day by Day: 1809–1865*. Dayton: Morningside, 1991.

Niven, John. *Gideon Welles—Lincoln's Secretary of the Navy*. New York: Oxford, 1973.

Parkes, Henry Bamford. *A History of Mexico*. Boston: Houghton Mifflin, 1969.

Parks, Joseph Howard. *General Edmund Kirby Smith, C.S.A.* Baton Rouge: 1962.

Parrish, T. Michael. *Richard Taylor: Soldier Prince of Dixie*. Chapel Hill: University of North Carolina Press, 1992.

Porter, Horace. *Campaigning With Grant*. Edited by Wayne C. Temple. Bloomington: Indiana University Press, 1961.

Randall, J. G. *Lincoln the President*. New York: Dodd Mead,1945–1955. 4 Vols.

Sears, Stephen W. *George B. McClellan: The Young Napoleon*. New York: Ticknor & Fields, 1988.

Sherman, William Tecumseh. *Memoirs of General W. T. Sherman*. With Notes by Charles Royster. New York: Library of America, 1990.

Tanner, Robert G. *Stonewall in the Valley*. Garden City: Doubleday, 1976.

Taylor, Richard. *Destruction and Reconstruction*. New York: D. Appleton, 1879. The edition used herein was published by Bantam Books in 1992.

Thomas, Benjamin P. and Harold M. Hyman. *Stanton: The Life and Times of Lincoln's Secretary of War*. New York: Knopf, 1962.

Trefousse, H. L. *Benjamin Franklin Wade: Radical Republican From Ohio*. New York: Twayne Publishers, 1963.

———. *The Radical Republicans: Lincoln's Vanguard for Racial Justice*. Baton Rouge: Louisiana State University Press, 1969.

U.S. Congress. Report of the Joint Committee on the Conduct of the War, 1863–1866. *Red River Expedition*. Millwood, NY: Kraus Reprint, 1977.

U.S. Navy Department. *Official Records of the Union and Confederate Navies in the War of the Rebellion*. Washington: Government Printing Office, 1894–1917. 27 vols.

War of the Rebellion: Official Records of the Union and Confederate Armies. Washington: Government Printing Office, 1880–1901. 70 Vols. in 128. Also used in this project was *The Civil War CD-ROM*, published in 1997 by Guild Press of Indiana, Inc., Carmel, IN.

Williams, Kenneth P. *Lincoln Finds a General*. 5 Vols. New York: Macmillan, 1949–1959.

Williams, T. Harry. *Lincoln and his Generals*. New York: Knopf, 1952.

———. *Lincoln and the Radicals*. Madison: University of Wisconsin Press, 1965.

INDEX

An asterisk (*) by a number indicates a photo on that page.